# The 'Glocalization' of Mobile Telephony in West and Central Africa:
## Consumer Appropriation and Corporate Acculturation
### *A Case Study in Cameroon and Guinea-Conakry*

## Max A. Smith

*Langaa Research & Publishing CIG*
*Mankon, Bamenda*

*Publisher:*
*Langaa* RPCIG
Langaa Research & Publishing Common Initiative Group
P.O. Box 902 Mankon
Bamenda
North West Region
Cameroon
Langaagrp@gmail.com
www.langaa-rpcig.net


Distributed in and outside N. America by African Books Collective
orders@africanbookscollective.com
www.africanbookscollective.com


*ISBN-10: 9956-550-39-6*

*ISBN-13: 978-9956-550-39-5*

© Max A. Smith 2018

*For Serge Atangana*

# Table of Contents

# Introduction

## Unexpected Twists and Turns

In the mid-1990s, an unsettling story was circulating in the northern communities of Togo. One night a plane landed at the Niamtougou airport which was built in the 1970s in a place notorious for its mystical powers. The man in charge of the airport – a European – was taken aback as he had not expected any aircraft that night. He approached the plane and found only Africans on board, who happened to be endowed with magical powers. They surrounded him and seized a book in which he had been writing. Then they released him, and the aircraft disappeared into the night (Piot 1999: 176).

In this tale, Africans with magical powers are in command of a technology that was invented by Westerners (the plane) and they are attempting to appropriate another of the colonizer's powers (the written word/books). Instead of killing the European and rejecting his technology, these technology-savy Africans make his powers their own. This story about power and appropriation relates well to the concepts that are explored in this book. Rather than interpreting the appropriation of mobile telephony as a form of rendition, a defeat, this study highlights the ways in which technology from the outside, mobile telephony, can be reconfigured and altered in locally meaningful ways through the processes of appropriation and acculturation.

Implicitly if not explicitly, scholars of Africa often associate the West with 'modernity' and Africa with 'tradition'. Sociologists, such as Max Weber, view societies organized on the basis of kinship – as is often the case in Africa – as preoccupied with the 'eternal yesterday' and therefore as tradition-bound and unchanging (Bates 2010: 15). Similarly, some anthropologists have categorized these societies as encapsulated in a 'timeless present,' as if the lives of their populations were suspended in time. Clichés of an immutable Africa circulate in the media, and the continent – less developed, by any measure, than other parts of the world – is widely regarded as 'lagging behind', with most of its countries failing to implement modernity's signature institutions (democracy, secularism, individualism, monogamous marriage). In this study of mobile telephony, however, I join other scholars of Africa in challenging both the entrenched dichotomy between tradition and modernity and the assumption of unilineal progress in human history.

Through first-hand experiences in Africa I have come to understand what V.S. Naipaul meant by 'people are the most creative when things are very perturbed' (French 2008: 273). Although, or perhaps because, sub-Saharan Africa is the poorest part of the world, people there are more 'globalized' than elsewhere. They speak of the 'international community' as if it were a real person; they live at once in different temporalities and navigate parallel universes; most of them are fluent in several languages; many are uprooted, flushed out of their villages into cities; their future is utterly unpredictable; nothing is predetermined, all is possible. I now liken this condition, and the ambivalent experience of permanent impermanence, to 'modernity' – as opposed to *The World of Yesterday,* Stefan Zweig's more stable and foreseeable future (Zweig 1942). African nations are not lagging behind, but are on a different plane, a place no other part of the world has been before. What I have learned in Africa takes me back to America with questions, modern questions I would not have asked myself otherwise, and which led me to undertake this research.

In the Fall of 2016, I set out for a study-abroad semester in Cameroon with the firm intention to find a research topic that would examine the capacity of individuals to lead their own lives and the resilience I associate with the continent, as well as the flaws at the heart of this resourcefulness. I had no particular interest in mobile phones, but during a previous visit to a village in Ivory Coast, I had been intrigued to find Androids and iPads where there was no electricity or running water. With this in mind, I landed in Yaoundé. Soon after my arrival, seeking to put credit on my phone, I was directed to a woman sitting under an umbrella by the roadside who appeared to be selling cigarettes, beignets, alcoholic drinks – just about everything but phone credit. Tentatively I walked over to her and, expecting to be laughed at, asked for credit. To my surprise, she pulled out three cellphones from her coat, asked for my phone number and how much money I needed. A few manipulations later, I received a text message alerting me to the fact that the sum I had paid had been received. The woman had not moved and barely spoken. All she had done was press a few buttons on one of her three phones and in a matter of seconds, the transaction was completed. I was baffled and greatly intrigued by this interaction. Over time, I came to understand not only that the booming mobile economy in Cameroon was grounded in local realities but, also, that it could serve as a medium to reveal African agency and resilience, i.e. the capacity of individuals to redefine their lives against the odds of overwhelming circumstances. Eventually, I would also become aware of the fact that this form of resistance by the global underdog comes at a price.

For the next four months, I familiarized myself with Cameroon, Cameroonians and the latter's uses of mobile telephony. I lived with five different host families hopping, for instance, from an apartment in Yaoundé with Wi-Fi-connection to a mud-hut in a village with no electricity. This book builds on these experiences, along with my studies at the School for International Training (SIT) in Yaoundé, which culminated in the form of a 65-page independent study project on the 'local appropriation' of mobile telephony and the modes of gaining ownership of a supposedly 'neutral' technology. For almost a decade, sub-Saharan Africa has been the fastest growing market for mobile telephony. Therefore, examining the ways in which local agency shapes the appropriation of this technology is a formidable window onto the contemporary realities of the continent. Aware of having only scratched the surface, I longed to deepen my understanding. During the summer of 2017, I obtained funding from my academic institution, Kenyon College, to further this study during a month-long internship with the international telephone company MTN in Guinea-Conakry. The aim was to conduct research on the 'corporate acculturation' of mobile telephony, i.e. the ways in which companies tailor their operations to consumer preferences and local realities. In the process of acculturation, designers and mobile operators display strategic agency in shaping the field, while in the process of appropriation Africans only exercise tactical agency in finding new uses for mobile phones within the field structured by others, even though at times they push back at the boundaries. This book combines my findings from Cameroon and Guinea in an effort to illustrate common features in the 'glocalization' of mobile telephony in West Africa.

While economic dimensions are often front and center in discourses on the 'mobile revolution' in sub-Saharan Africa, this research is primarily of a Cultural Studies nature as it focuses on cultural aspects of global interactions and social changes. It adds to a growing body of research studying technological adoption as a direct outcome of socioeconomic needs and behavior in the developing world. In sub-Saharan Africa, more people have mobile phones than access to electricity, yet they find ways to charge their devices, which I explore in Chapter 2, and to adapt them to their needs.[1] Analyzing the uses of mobile phones south of the Sahara is particularly important in light of the demographics of the region. Between 1960 and 2010 the population of sub-Saharan Africa quadrupled from 230 million to over 1 billion. In 2050, out of a total of 10 billion people in the world, 25% will be Africans. While there will be 450 million aging Europeans, there will be 2.5 billion Africans, two-thirds of them below the age of thirty (Smith 2018: 19, 45). In 2100, these numbers are expected to double, of 11 billion people worldwide, 40% will be Africans. Never before in human history has a region of the world been as young as sub-Saharan Africa is today. As a consequence, at least demographically speaking, the adoption of mobile phones by Africans matters as they represent a rapidly growing segment of the world population and will increasingly shape the use of the technology in the future.

This book begins with a brief historical reminder of the emergence of 'glocalization' as a concept in the 1990s. The first chapter interrogates the presumptive neutrality of technology and provides definitions of 'appropriation' and 'acculturation' within the realm of mobile telephony, as well as a timeline for the rapid expansion of mobile telephony in West Africa. The second chapter draws upon a case study in Cameroon to illustrate how local agency trumps the neutrality of a means of communication in the process of consumer appropriation. It examines the ways in which Cameroonians have taken ownership of the informal cellular economy and explores consumptive and creative forms of appropriation by consumers. The third chapter draws from research conducted at MTN in Guinea-Conakry in order to contrast consumer appropriation of mobile telephony with corporate acculturation. It evaluates the role of mobile telephony companies in the 'glocalization' of mobile phones. In particular, it illustrates the ways in which these corporations adapt their offers and strategies to local realities, while at the same time, shaping the environment in which the consumer appropriates the technology. The fourth and concluding chapter, summarizes the manner in which consumer appropriation (bottom-up) and corporate acculturation (top-down) combine to shape the glocalization of mobile telephony in West Africa, and the attendant benefits. However, it challenges the Information and Communication Technology for Development (ICT4D) narratives which are rooted in a stage model of ascendant progress and present mobile phones as a panacea for the development of sub-Saharan Africa. The conclusion of this book address the underlying tension at play between 'globalizers' and 'globalized' in the spread of mobile telephony in West Africa and points out directions for future research.

## Notes

1    'In Much of Sub-Saharan Africa, Mobile Phones Are More Common than Access to Electricity'. *The Economist* Newspaper, 8 Nov. 2017.

# Chapter 1

## Terminology and Literature Review

### A. 'Glocalization' – A Brief History of the Concept

Humans have always engaged in cultural exchanges, the dissemination of knowledge, and the trade of goods and services between different regions. Sub-Saharan Africa actively participated in the Indian Ocean trade networks with Asia and the Middle East from around 600 A.D to the mid-16th century as well as in the trans-Saharan caravan trade connecting it with the Mediterranean world. With the invention of the caravel in the 15th century, which allowed Europeans to sail against the wind, trade between the Old continent and Africa intensified. However, Africans have often been victimized by globalizing policies of Western powers, first during the transatlantic slave trade, which was most intense between 1650 and 1800, and then under colonial rule after the Berlin Conference of 1884/85 (Cheru 2002: 2). Overall, the pursuit of economic opportunities around the globe has driven merchants and states for a long time, but certain periods in history stand out for the intensity of global investments and trade. It was not until the early 1990s that the concept of globalization in economics and the social sciences became an increasingly influential paradigm, understood not just as border-crossing interactions but as a global phenomenon of a worldwide 'now-time', where it matters to all parts of the globe what is taking place somewhere else.

Although opinions vary, the conventional view emerging out of the Western scholarly literature identifies three broad eras of globalization. Most scholars, most notably renowned sociologist Immanuel Wallerstein in *The Modern World System*, label the first era of globalization as starting in 1492 – when Columbus opened trade between the Old and New World – up until the beginning

1

globalization not synonymous with Westernization and the need to acknowledge the agency of non-Europeans in the process. International exchanges such as the Indian Ocean trade networks were not globalization as we understand it today, but they portray how fragmentation (the suppression of space by time), hybridity and other buzzwords for post-modernism are not specific to a certain time period (Cooper 2000: 316). The world was interconnected during the transatlantic slave trade in the 16th and 17th century, and colonialism was also a form of globalization which led to a dense network of multi-layered interdependence as early as the 1920s to a degree which was only attained again in the 1990s – when the concept of globalization was coined. Therefore, Jeffrey Sachs and others can be challenged in their belief that Africa has been 'by-passed' by globalization. Rather, the continent is globalizing in singular ways, parting *The World of Yesterday*, sometimes by being globalized as evidenced in its adoption of mobile phones. The birth of globalization as a concept is recent. For the purpose of this study it is most relevant to examine how the concept has gradually expanded beyond an emphasis on economics and has reinterpreted the interpenetration of the global and the local, as expressed in the concept of 'glocalization'.

It was not until the early 1990s that the concept of globalization in economics and the social sciences became a dominant paradigm. Following the end of the Cold War, the Communist bloc fell apart and its former member states began to integrate into the global market economy. A new degree of interaction between nations emerged. Liberal-minded economists contended that the more countries let market forces rule and open their economies to free trade and competition, the more efficient and thriving their economies will be (Friedman 2000: 11). Globalization entails the universal adoption of free-market capitalism – opening, deregulating and privatizing national economies – and the spread of a market-driven dominant homogenizing culture. The end of the Cold War marked an increase in international trade and investment and the lowering of migration barriers between the capitalist West and former Communist nations. There were notable exceptions such as the economies of Russia, North Korea, Vietnam, Mianmar, and China, which remain under state control to this day. In various shapes and forms, we know now that globalization greatly intensified without triumphing worldwide. Nonetheless, back in the 1990s a wave of optimism spread through the ranks of Western economists. They believed that this emerging era of free trade and competition, i.e. the 'age of globalization', would open even more foreign markets, stimulate exports in goods and services, and bring economic growth and prosperity for most of the planet. The 'non-aligned world' would also embrace globalization as markets, finance and technologies would shrink space and time, and an unprecedented era of prosperity, innovation, and collaboration would ensue (Friedman 2005, 8).

Influenced by this wave of optimism and in an effort to adapt to the 'New World Order', sociologists sought to move away from their previously narrow conceptualization of boxed-in societies and to interpret society on a global scale (Khondker 2004: 2). Prior to the 1990s, the field of sociology had been criticized, most notably by Anthony Giddens and Immanuel Wallerstein, for its focus on bounded societies and the study of modern nation-states. However, in the 1990s Roland Robertson, a British-American sociologist, spearheaded a movement to redefine the scope of sociology as the study of global social processes. In 1992, Robertson was the first to define globalization as a 'compression of the world and the intensification of consciousness of the world as a whole. In thought and action, it makes the world a single place' (Robertson 1992: 8). In other words, Robertson argued that globalization encompasses the concomitant interaction of different regions of the world, having previously lived, so to speak, in different time zones, to promote global interdependence.

This emerging consciousness was particularly enhanced by technological advances in communication, such as the advent of the internet and mobile phones, as well as free trade agreements instituting open markets and global competitiveness. By the beginning of the 21$^{st}$ century, the concept of globalization was subject to various interpretations but widely understood as referring to the process of making the world a more interconnected place through the intensification of technological, political, economic, and cultural exchanges between peoples and across international boundaries. However, critics – in particular many anthropologists – challenged this homogenizing vision for its denial of all local particularity and the creation of a false sense of connectedness. Furthermore, the lofty predictions of economists faced the backlash of developing nations which denounced the neo-liberal and free-market capitalistic system as primarily advantageous to Western nations. Globalization was increasingly interpreted as being a Western-defined 'modernity' and a political project aimed to center the West and marginalize the rest.

In *Global Modernities* (1995), Robertson and other sociologists argue that globalization preceded modernity and is not one of its consequences. Robertson contends that this ambiguity stems from mistakenly associating *globalization* with the triumphant march of modernity across the world, whereas *globality* points to a widening space – the global – that is being filled by different civilizations or sites of modernity. Robertson seeks to 'deconstruct' modernity and globalization, by de-centering the world - i.e. knocking the West out of its center. While the concept of globalization implies the development of a global consciousness, it does not equate with global consensus. Some prefer to view the world as an assembly of distinct communities, while others believe in a single overarching organization with the best interests of humanity as a whole in mind.

In a world ever more interconnected, the coexistence of differing world views allows for mutual enrichment as much as it can cause cultural clashes – the balance between the two being tipped by global power relationships (see Barber 1995; Huntington 1997). Globalization – as a framework for a geopolitical and macro-sociological context – is not best suited for the study of social realities on the ground, which mingle the particular and the universal. There cannot be a 'local' that is not also 'global'. Globalization is refracted locally into singular forms. The two depend on each other and constantly redefine each other. This is why, for example, romantic views of the village in Africa as a site of traditional culture – an 'out-site' or a place to locate the Other – err in conjuring up an impossible outside of the global system. They overlook the fact that such sites are being shaped by the modern but have also played a role – even if limited – in shaping it. They are 'remotely global', the apposite title of Charles Piot's book about: 'Village Modernity in West Africa'. In it, Piot draws lessons from his long field work in northern Togo, in a village – Kuwdwé – near the town of Kara. In Kudwé, Pentecostal revivalism has upended the spiritual world, both rivaling and fueling witchcraft beliefs, and male adolescents abandon their families for the 'adventure' of seasonal migration to Nigeria, where they work much harder than at home in plantations to bring back a cheap Chinese or Indian motorcycle, proof of their newly gained 'independence'. Meantime, their parents listen to Radio France International (RFI) or the BBC while drinking sorghum beer or palm wine. In short, there is no daylight between the local and the global, tradition and modernity. It is this insight which led Robertson, along with anthropologists, to posit that the universal and the particular can and should be combined under a new umbrella term: '*glocalization*'.

In the 1990s, Robertson introduced this neologism into Western social-scientific discourse to illustrate the duality of global processes and the extent to which both global and local are mutually constituent realities that cannot be understood in isolation from each other. The state of societies and their future are not determined solely by macro-level forces but also by groups, organizations and individuals operating at the micro level (Roudometof 2016: 12). Effectively, the concept of 'glocalization' recognizes the agency of individuals at the local level and their ability to redefine the field in which outside influences can enrich their culture and economy. The 'glocal' offers a resolution to contentious characteristics and questions associated with globalization, such as the relationship between heterogeneity and homogeneity or the distinction between modernization and globalization.

In the context of technologies, 'glocalization' refers to goods and services produced for a global market which comprises many local markets. Glocalization encompasses the mobile telephony sector in West Africa in that mobile telecommunication operators purchase mobile phones from foreign companies, such as Huawei, Tecno Mobile, and Nokia. In a little over a decade, cellular penetration in sub-Saharan Africa surged from almost nil to around 420 million unique mobile subscribers, yet not a single African company manufactures mobile phones on a large scale.[2] The large majority of mobile phones in West Africa are manufactured abroad, most often at cheap costs in China before being purchased in the commercial center of Dubai, and brought to Africa where they are appropriated and acculturated to fit the needs and local realities of societies. The following section interrogates the presumptive neutrality of technology and the extent to which mobile phones manufactured abroad retain their alterity.

## B. The Presumptive Neutrality of Technology

Philosopher Kwame Anthony Appiah, in his 1991 article 'Is the Post- in Postmodernism the Post- in Postcolonial?' focuses on a piece labeled *Yoruba Man with a Bicycle* in an exhibition shown in New York in 1987. James Baldwin, one of the curators of the event organized by the Center for African Art, had chosen this sculpture despite the apparent influences of the Western world on the Yoruba man, both in the clothes he wears and the bicycle he sits on. Appiah praises Baldwin for identifying a piece which was not in the mold of African 'primitivism' and displayed the hybridization that results from the intermingling of cultures. As Appiah explains, the artist who produced the Yoruba man with a bicycle 'does not care that the bicycle is the white man's invention: it is not there to be Other to the Yoruba Self; it is there because someone cared for its solidity; it is there because it will take us further than our feet will take us; it is there because machines are now as African as novelists' (Appiah 1991: 357). Appiah rejects the notion of a fully homegrown *pure* African culture. As a result of the transformative nature of globalization, the bicycle has been appropriated to become an African machine. In the same vein, mobile telephony has been appropriated and acculturated to become an African 'thing' corresponding to local needs and realities, and reshaping them in turn. Rather than interpreting such appropriations as a capitulation to Western modes of life, this research joins that of other scholars to illustrate how society and technology in West Africa condition themselves mutually (De Bruijn et al. 2009: 12). Nonetheless, online spaces are spheres of influence for governments, corporations and individuals (Nyamnjoh et al. 2016: 7) and given that mobile phones are not locally produced sub-Saharan Africa depends on 'technology transfer' and foreign 'know-how'. Hence, at the heart of the tension between 'globalizers' and 'globalized' lies the question of whether mobile telephony can truly be neutral if it is the result of concrete activities and products of enquiring human beings.

In Appiah's interpretation of the *Yoruba Man with a Bicycle*, technology is neutral. A tool or technology is a means to an end, which awaits the animation of a human purpose and cannot be 'good' or 'evil' as it has no thoughts or desires of its own (Blacker 1994: 297). As such, mobile phones, by themselves, have no independent causative power and simply 'handle information in digital format. That's all' (Heeks 2002, 3). Technology is here posited as 'neutral' insofar as it can belong equally to those who invented it and to those who tailor it to their needs. Accordingly, 'Western' ideas and inventions such as mobile phones do not remain Western but are 'glocalized' – if they were ever 'Western' to begin with, considering that their birth certificates are always co-signed. This commonsense picture of means-ends relationships resembles what philosopher Langdon Winner has coined 'straight-line instrumentalism', i.e. the concept that 'neutral tools are brought to bear on ends that are valued for reasons external to the situations within which the tools have been developed' (Hickman 1990, 202). However, the notion that technology constitutes a value-neutral tool merely used to contribute to human desire, has been criticized within the humanities and has been widely challenged by philosophers who consider it to be a form of 'naïve instrumentalism'.

My case studies in Cameroon and Guinea demonstrate the local agency of consumers and mobile operators in tailoring mobile telephony to local needs. Nonetheless, Africa is incorporated into the global technological revolution in a dependent manner – as an importer, rather than producer of mobile phones, as a user rather than an inventor (Murphy and Carmody 2015: 211). This has led many African intellectuals to be wary of the spread of mobile phones which, in their eyes, may result in the loss of 'cultural identity' (Binsbergen 2004). Accordingly, what is Western or Asian about mobile telephony should be questioned, just as what is African about Africa should be a question and not an assumption (Cooper 2000: 309). In his critique of technology, particularly in his *magnum opus Experience and Nature,* philosopher John Dewey rejects all forms of historical or economic determinism advanced by Karl Marx and the notion of a 'will' that can be either free or bound. Dewey's central claim is that technology does not function as a neutral means towards externally assigned ends but that technologies are 'inextricably woven into the fabric of human life' (Blacker 1994:

298). It is evident that mobile phones, as a non-living object, have no 'core', but Dewey rejects the notion that a means can be interpreted in radical isolation from the end it serves. In *Mobilities, ICTs and Marginality in Africa* (2016), Francis Nyamnjoh and other anthropologists argue that humans and mobile phones are increasingly two sides to the same coin and that 'the online' and 'the offline' – i.e. the physical and virtual – combine to form an inseparable realm rather than distinctive spaces (Nyamnjoh et al. 2016: 17). Drawing on Dewey's thoughts, mobile telephony could be viewed as formed by the desires of Westerners before, in turn, shaping their desires.

If mobile phones were manufactured in sub-Saharan Africa, they would most likely be solar-powered or have more extensive battery life – given the lack of electricity and the frequency of power outages – than the ones currently imported from Asia and Europe. This not being the case, mobile phones have not been 'reinvented' south of the Sahara but appropriated in ways unforeseen by their creators. This research finds that, though mobile phones are a globalizing technology, their spread doesn't mean that foreign desires are shaping African desires, nor should they be perceived as a new 'colonizing' or alienating force. However, the larger and crucial issue raised by Dewey – can human agency override the predetermined usage of a technology, or is it conditioned by the technology? – remains an open question.

In the second half of the 20th century, Jacques Ellul dismissed the neutralist idea that the effects of technology – good or bad – depend on *how* humans use it (Chandler 2014). According to Ellul, technologies or tools, like a knife, carry a number of positive and negative consequences which are separate from human intention but which lead humans to be conditioned by their technological inventions (Ellul 1990). Ellul's theory supports the claim explored in chapter two that mobile phones are ruining marriages in Cameroon and that infidelity is enabled by mobile phones. Moreover, mobile phones liberate humans from certain physical constraints, but they also subject them to abstract ones (Ellul 1990: 325). Ellul argues that, as humans increasingly act through intermediaries, they lose touch with reality. For example, the increased use of the clock in the 14th century improved efficiency and the coordination of man's daily activities, but as Ellul argues in support of Lewis Mumford's thoughts in *Technics and Civilization* (1934), instead of *living* time, man is now split up and parceled by it (Mumford 1934: 13-18). Likewise, one could contend that mobile telephony is not simply a tool created by man to surpass himself but becomes his second nature through an autonomous and repetitive process to which its users are subjected. According to this line of thought, mobile phones are not neutral as they shape a new environment for humans and modify man's very essence as well as his view of the world. In the *Surrender of Culture to Technology* (1993), psychologist Neil Postman claims that to 'a man with a pencil, everything looks like a list' – which echoes the saying, most often attributed to Abraham Maslow, that to someone with only a hammer the world looks like a nail (Postman 1993: 14). But, if mobile phones have pre-conditioned usages to which humans are subjected, then how can we explain their drastic variations in the use made of them across different parts of the world?

Despite similarities in discourse with the aforementioned theorists, Dewey is more nuanced in his analysis and does not present technology as autonomous. Dewey acknowledges that a technology, or a 'thing', is neutral in itself as it needs some context of involvement in order to obtain value and that such value varies depending on the needs of human beings. Things like a rock or a cup do not have an ontological property or value of their own. Nonetheless, the 'straight-line instrumentalist' approach views technologies as an unchanging means to an end, while for Dewey technology cannot be reduced to an aggregation of devices. Technologies, like the bicycle of the Yoruba man and mobile phones, can become *embodied* in such a way that it is hard to decipher where the self ends and the tool begins (Blacker 1994: 307). Mobile phones are 'non-living' objects but when used by humans within specific social contexts they can change the course of actions made by human agents, implicating their agency yet not indicating their control over humans. Mobile phones are neither all powerful nor entirely malleable to social shaping by consumers appropriating them (Nyamnjoh et al. 2016: 2-5). Based on this understanding, it would be naïve to consider mobile telephony as value-neutral, merely instrumental, or even asocial, as it is a product of the scientific inquiries, desires and needs of humans outside of Africa.

The global and the local redefine and depend on each other, but globalization does not originate from a multitude of 'locals'. Rather, globalization is refracted locally and takes on local forms, as demonstrated in the 'glocalization' of mobile telephony in West Africa. A villager in Nyakokombo lives in a 'remotely global' place, but he has not shaped modernity like, for example, a New Yorker. Rather he has mostly been 're-shaped' by a modernity in places like New York, Beijing or Paris. This concept, however, does not exclude that a technology like the clock does not take the pulsating rhythm out of life but, rather, the pulse of life changes with the technology that humans invent. While humans and Information Communication Technologies (ICTs) increasingly intertwine to shape social relations and society, mobile phones are dependent on human enablers and are 'as accommodating as they are accommodated' by users (Nyamnjoh et al. 2016: 27). The measure of things – of speed, performance, progress… – is always the human being. However, it is not always the same human being, because with the technology we invent and apply, we reinvent ourselves. Accordingly, mobile telephony must be understood within its specific social contexts, which means that its value can be altered depending on the setting.

Rather than mere *mimicry*, in their adoption of mobile phones, populations in West Africa engage in *mimesis*. *Mimesis* can be defined as 'the nature that culture uses to create second nature, the faculty to copy, imitate, make models, explore difference, yield into and become Other' (Taussig 1993: xiii). It is the simultaneity of *mimesis* and *alterity* that is at the source of glocalization. Mobile telephony – like a palimpsest – should not be discussed without acknowledging the traces of Western and Asian influence and the tension of 'globalizers versus globalized'. However, the agency exercised in the consumer appropriation (bottom-up) and the corporate acculturation (top-down) of the technology in West Africa, has led mobile telephony to rapidly become embodied in local societies. Throughout West Africa and the wider sub-Saharan region, mobile telephony is a 'globalizing' technology but not a vector of assimilation to Westernization, as it is refigured in locally meaningful ways to fit local needs and realities. The 'glocalization' of mobile telephony is not a panacea for the development of sub-Saharan Africa, and inherent flaws lie at the heart of the resourcefulness portrayed in my case studies, yet it is a testament to Africans overcoming seemingly fixed limitations of use and to be active agents rather than collateral victims of globalization.

## C. Game of Mirrors: Appropriation and Acculturation

### a. *Appropriation*

The term appropriation derives from the Latin verb *appropriare* – 'to make one's own' (Krings 2015: 16). It is linked to ownership, and the legislative act authorizing the expenditure of public funds, and is frequently brought up in studies about authorship, copyright, and intellectual property as well as debates on the restitution and protection of 'cultural property'. In the 1980s, the field of postcolonial studies emerged in the United States and birthed the concept of 'cultural appropriation' as a new dimension in the critique of subordinate relations and, in particular, colonialism. The term suggests the 'theft' of cultural practices 'belonging' to historically oppressed groups by colonial or postcolonial powers. However, in recent years the concept has resurfaced and gained the broader connotation of the pillage of other cultures by the Western world, often thought of as 'white'.

In its contemporary use, 'cultural appropriation' implies an imbalance of power and forms of domination and exploitation where elements are copied and used outside of their original cultural context. It has developed into a militant argument and justifies outcries over whites sporting dreadlocks or wearing sombreros at themed parties on college campuses, fiction writers developing characters of another 'race', white painter Dana Schutz laying claim to the cultural heritage of the civil rights movement in her painting of Emmet Till, or Elvis Presley for drawing inspiration from the rhythm and blues of black American musicians. On the other hand, when Barbara Hendricks, a black soprano, sings the Ave Maria composed by Frantz Schubert, a white Austrian, she does not face the same backlash. As Bruce Ziff and Pratima Rao contend in their introduction to *Borrowed Power: Essays on Cultural Appropriation* (1997), appropriation is primarily an act of taking from a subordinate to enrich an already dominant culture. On the contrary, appropriations by the 'oppressed' should not be denounced because they should be seen as 'cultural assimilation'. Ziff and Rao draw a clear dividing line between the 'oppressed and their 'oppressors', to whom they lend hereditary status, and their conception of culture suggests that cultural goods have identifiable and exclusive inventors and owners. Their idea of sealed cultures conflicts with the viewpoints not only of historians like Frederick Cooper but also of anthropologists who have specialized in Africa, like Matthias Krings, Francis Nyamnjoh and Charles Piot. The latter provide the basis for the conception of appropriation developed in this book.

In *African Appropriations*, Krings acknowledges the importance of discussing the power relationships at play in the politics of appropriation. He takes issue, however, with Ziff and Rao's terminology and their interpretation of 'cultural appropriation' and 'cultural assimilation'. First, Ziff and Rao are defining a single practice – that is taking something out of one context and putting it into another – by two different names. Second, 'cultural assimilation' supposes a conception of *culture* as a bounded and homogeneous body to which 'intruding' elements need to be assimilated (Krings 2015: 17). These extraneous if not alien elements must be stripped of their otherness, or alterity, not to imperil the purported cultural purity and homeostasis of these societies. In short, Ziff and Rao argue that 'hegemonic groups' *appropriate* objects as they value alterity and wish to retain the difference or 'exotic' nature of the item, whereas 'subaltern groups' *assimilate* as they wish to get rid of the otherness of the object or practice incorporated into their culture. Krings disputes this conceptualization arguing that it grants considerably less agency to those who 'assimilate' than those who 'appropriate'. In the context of Africa, Ziff and Rao's understanding of cultural assimilation is problematic as it reduces the adoption of Western culture to mere mimicry and presents Africans as passive victims of 'cultural imperialism' (Krings 2015: 19). In doing so, it denies the agency and creativity of appropriation, as well as it supposes the existence of a distinct African identity. Nyamnjoh warns against reasoning in terms of 'permanent victors' and 'permanent victims', as such notions miss out on the 'nuanced complexities' in a world of circulation and interconnection rather than bounded and discrete identities (Nyamnjoh et al. 2016: 2). Krings and Nyamnjoh do not claim that appropriation necessarily subverts the alien original, but they differentiate mimicry from mimesis.

Both mimicry and mimesis share the same Greek root, *mimos*, the 'imitator' or 'mime' – not by coincidence an actor. The basis of mimesis theory and the ambiguity which comes with the practice dates back to the works of Plato, *The Republic* (380 BC), and Aristotle, *Poetics* (360-320 BC). Since, the concept of mimesis has expanded from its original meaning as the 'imitation of animals and humans in speech, song, or dance' to imitative representation writ large while mimicry has emerged as a term to denote flawed colonial mimesis. Postcolonial theorists – building on Frantz Fanon's *Black Skin, White Masks* (1952) – have associated mimicry of Euro-American cultural practices as the expression of an inferiority complex expressed by black people living under colonial conditions. In contrast, mimesis stands for an attempt to participate in the imitated and entails 'repetition [appropriation] with a difference' (Piot 2010: 129). In *Remotely Global* (1999), Charles Piot rejects the association between local appetite for foreign goods and a Western type of colonization. Rather, Piot views the process as creative appropriations – or 'cannibalizations' – of the cultural inventory of the West. A decade later, Piot revisits the concept of cultural mimesis in *Nostalgia for the Future* (2010) and highlights the agency of the 'local', i.e. Africans who, ironically, reject a past coded 'African' in the appropriation of Euro-otherness. Piot's analysis builds upon Michael Taussig's *Mimesis and Alterity* (1993), to display how Africans do not simply assimilate but appropriate foreign norms, items or technologies and refigure them in locally meaningful ways while retaining aspects of their alterity. It is this kindred intricacy of mimesis and alterity that is at the heart of my understanding of 'glocalization'.

With this in mind, the following chapter on the local appropriation of mobile telephony in Cameroon nuances the interpretation of mobile telephony, and more generally ICTs, as both a tool of Western hegemony and a silver bullet for development. It operates under the working-definition of 'consumer appropriation' as a process whereby an object is re-interpreted, adapted or even re-invented by those who are out of the vicinity of its original production. However, 'consumer appropriation' represents only half of the equation to understanding how mobile telephony is (re)shaping social realities in African societies and how Africans societies are in turn shaping this technology of communication. To grasp the 'glocalization' of mobile telephony in West Africa, it is equally important to examine the effects of the 'corporate acculturation' of mobile telephony.

## b. Acculturation

The term 'acculturation' is often employed interchangeably with 'assimilation', yet they differ in many ways. Sociologists tend to use the latter, while most anthropologists prefer the former. The original definition of acculturation was offered by Robert Redfield, Ralph Linton, and Melville Herskovits, three anthropologists, in *Memorandum for the Study of Acculturation* (1936). It referred to 'those phenomena which result when groups or individuals having different cultures come into continuous first-hand contact, with subsequent changes in the original patterns of either or both groups' (Redfield et al. 1936: 149). Building on this definition, acculturation is broadly understood as a dynamic process – as opposed to a single event – of adaptation to new conditions of life and the adoption of cultural traits or social patterns of another group (Teske and Bardin 1974: 2). In *Acculturation and Assimilation* (1974), Teske and Bardin provide a conceptual framework to differentiate the two concepts. They find acculturation to be a necessary condition for assimilation but also an independent process which can unfold independently without leading to assimilation. Hence, Teske and Bardin define assimilation as a uni-directional process which lacks the freedom and flexibility of acculturation. Whereas assimilation suggests that change can only occur in a single direction with one group becoming increasingly like the other, acculturation regards transformation as a mutual or reciprocal process between groups. Since 'identity' is not a product but a production, it's an ongoing, never-ending process, hence it's fluidity. The incorporation of newness/modernity into 'traditional culture' is a necessity, and happens all the time. When the 'traditional culture' incorporates previously extraneous elements, it is not 'maintained' as it used to be – it becomes something different, something new. There is loss involved, inexorably, as the new replaces parts of the old, or alters it.

In *Immigration, Acculturation, and Adaptation* (1997), psychologist John Berry counters this interpretation as he contends that assimilation is actually one of the many phases of acculturation. According to Berry, cultural groups may choose to employ either assimilation, separation, integration, or marginalization in the process of determining how best to acculturate to diverse settings. From this perspective, *acculturation* is not a step towards *assimilation* but rather the overarching process. Based on research analyzing the conceptualization of both terms within the social sciences, fellow psychologist David Sam supports the idea that acculturation is a more encompassing concept than assimilation (Sam 2006). In *The Forms of Capital* (1986), Pierre Bourdieu was the first to point out the role of intercultural communication in fostering what he coined 'cultural capital' (Bourdieu 1986: 241-258). Bourdieu understood cultural capital to be a set of skills, knowledge, and practices that give individuals power other than economic and political (Tran 2013: 21). In his view, the exchange of cultural capital through intercultural communication is intrinsically linked to the process of acculturation. Since the advent of modern ICTs towards the end of the 20th century, scholars have explored how these technological advances have transfigured cultural transactions. In *Disjuncture and Difference in the Global Cultural Economy* (1990), anthropologist Arjun Appadurai examines how the world has 'entered into an altogether new condition of neighborliness' and studies the ways in which ICTs have introduced greater complexity to global interactions, making cultures and societies more hybrid than ever before (Appadurai 1990: 2). Consequently, 'corporate acculturation' as explored in the third chapter of this book and the case study of MTN in Guinea-

Conakry, refer to the process by which mobile telephony companies adapt a globalizing technology and their operations, e.g. marketing and sales, to the cultural traits or social patterns of the country they operate in.

## D. The Leapfrog of Mobile Telephony in Sub-Saharan Africa

On April 3, 1973, the first mobile phone call was made when Martin Cooper, a senior engineer at Motorola, called rival telecommunication company Nokia and informed them he was speaking via a mobile phone.[3] The phone Cooper used to call weighed 1.1 kg (2.4 lbs), allowed 30 minutes of talk time and took 10 hours to charge.[4] In 1983, Motorola released its first commercial mobile phone for U.S. $4,000, and by 2003 the total number of mobile phone subscriptions worldwide surpassed the number of landline subscriptions.[5] Since 2015, mobile subscriptions outnumber the world's population.[6] While in high-income nations mobile phones became more practical in size and gained popularity amongst the general public during the 1990s, its spread south of the Sahara began only in earnest with the 21st century.

The appropriation of mobile telephony in sub-Saharan Africa is rooted in the unprecedented way that this new technology was adopted by the region. For lack of infrastructure, i.e. the landlines installed in most other parts of the world prior to mobile telephony, nations south of the Sahara skipped a stage and 'leapfrogged' directly from an almost non-existent fixed telephony grid to mobile connection. In 2000, Manhattan alone had more telephone lines than all of sub-Saharan African nations combined, and, even in the absence of mobile phones, the fixed telephone subscription in sub-Saharan Africa had never surpassed 1.6% (Stanton 2012: 371). In most countries, the scarcity of landlines was due to the inefficacy of the mostly state-run telecommunications sector. Where landlines existed in the first place, lack of maintenance, or the tropical climate, degraded this infrastructure. Historically, telephone poles in Cameroon were exposed not only to tropical storms but also to elephants rubbing against them and during colonial times, a first form of 'appropriation' of telephony was limited to stealing copper wires to be used as body ornaments (Nkwi 2009: 55-56). In 2000, fixed line subscribers only accounted for 0.6% of the Cameroonian population and 0.3% of the population in Guinea.[7] In the 2000s, however, government-owned telecommunication companies throughout sub-Saharan Africa were progressively superseded by private mobile telephony operators (MTN, Orange, Vodafone, Nextel, Airtel, etc.). With increased competition and evolving regulatory policies, the costs of telecommunications were reduced and service quality improved in equal measure. Over the following decade, the telephone, a tool and status symbol previously reserved for the elite, became the inseparable companion of the commoner.

Technological leapfrogging, an expression first used by Edward Steinmueller in 2001, is widely understood in the literature to be a process of 'bypassing stages in capacity building or investment through which countries were previously required to pass during the process of economic development' (Steinmueller 2001: 194). This definition aligns with Walt Whitman Rostow's theory of development as a linear pathway with well-defined stages (Rostow 1962). While this perception of economic growth is now highly disputed at the macroeconomic level, it remains prominent at the level of individual firms and industries due to the evidence that technological progress is cumulative and incremental (Steinmueller 2001: 194). Leapfrogging is particularly prevalent in the ICT4D discourse, as low-income countries may be able to leapfrog older vintages of technology to 'catch up' with developed countries and bridge the 'digital divide'. Low-income countries with the least commitment to the older technological infrastructure, such as landlines, have the most to gain from this qualitative leap. Accordingly, it comes with little surprise that 'leapfrogging' is frequent in Asia and Latin America and that Africa is the first part of the world where mobile phones have overtaken the number of fixed-line phones.[8]

In 2001, the prevalence of mobile cellular subscription in sub-Saharan Africa stood at only 2% (see Figure 1). In 2016, it had risen to around 75%. Put differently, the number of mobile

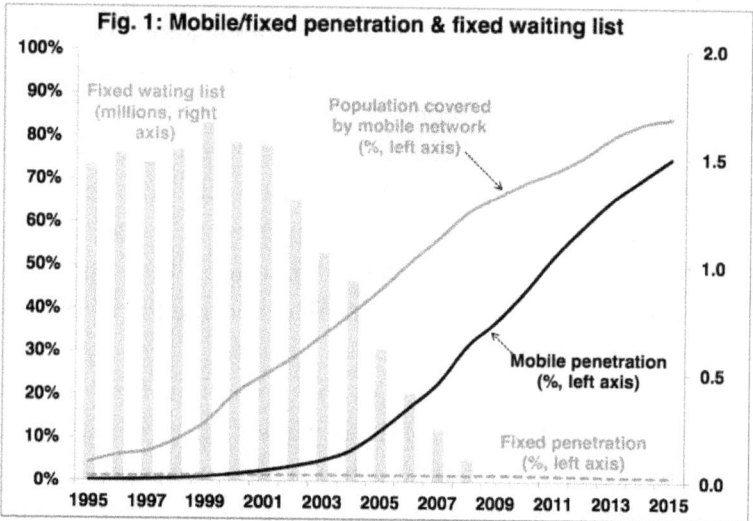

**Fig. 1: Mobile/fixed penetration & fixed waiting list**

Figure 1. Mobile/fixed penetration rates in sub-Saharan Africa

subscribers rose from around 17,000 to 750 million in fifteen years for a population of approximately 1 billion people.[9] Africa's mobile phone market is now the second largest in the world behind Asia and in the span of five years, between 2008 and 2012, internet bandwidth grew twentyfold with thousands of miles of cables having been laid across the continent.[10] By the end of 2016, there were 172 million unique subscribers in West Africa, accounting for 320 million mobile connections.[11] The region's subscriber penetration rate stood at 49%, slightly higher than the 47% penetration rate across Sub-Saharan Africa. Over the next four years, West Africa is expected to see an average subscriber growth of 6%, one of the highest globally, which will result in an additional 45 million subscribers by 2020. This growth is primarily due to countries like Ghana, where cellphone ownership rose from 8% to 83% from 2002 to 2016, and Nigeria, the biggest market south of the Sahara, where mobile phones have become as common as they are in the United States.[12] This technological leapfrog, often referred to as a 'mobile revolution', has garnered much attention as increased connectivity and telecommunication infrastructure are supposed to correlate with economic growth. Many scholars and politicians have hailed the advent of mobile telephony as the key to the economic emergence of sub-Saharan Africa and argued that 'technological leapfrogging' will narrow gaps in productivity and output separating industrialized and developing countries. Others, however, warn against such lofty predictions on the basis that one must learn how to walk before he can run.

Considering that mobile phones are not produced in sub-Saharan Africa, little progress has been made by the region at the technological 'frontier', i.e. the invention of new knowledge and capabilities. Nations south of the Sahara are dependent on 'technology transfer'. This concept suggests that firms in low-income countries can rapidly upgrade their capabilities by a suitable acquisition of equipment and 'know-how'. This process, however, is difficult for many reasons, among them the fact that a technology rarely stands independently and relies upon a variety of complementary technologies, or that intellectual property rights often prohibit the reproduction of technologies. Another argument particularly relevant to this research is that technologies are a means to an end and that the marketing for, and use of, the technology may differ substantially based on the local environment. It is this adaptation to local particularities that is explored in Cameroon and Guinea. The two case studies depict the current ways that West Africans and mobile operators have shaped the technology through consumer appropriation and corporate acculturation and how, in turn, mobile telephony has reshaped West African societies and corporate habits.

# Notes

2    GSMA. *The Mobile Economy – sub-Saharan Africa, 2017,* 11.

3    Zachary M. Seward, 'The First Mobile Phone Call Was Made 40 Years Ago Today.' *The Atlantic,* Atlantic Media Company, 3 Apr. 2013.

4    Richard Goodwin, 'The History of Mobile Phones from 1973 to 2008: The Handsets That Made It ALL Happen.' *Know Your Mobile,* Know Your Mobile, 6 Mar. 2017.

5    Tim Fernholz. 'More People around the World Have Cell Phones than Ever Had Land-Lines.' *Quartz,* Quartz, 25 Feb. 2014.

6    Felix Richter, 'Infographic: Mobile Subscriptions to Outnumber the World's Population.' *Statista Infographics,* 17 Nov. 2015.

7    'Fixed-Telephone Subscriptions (per 100 People).' *World Bank Data.*

8    For more on the leapfrogging of mobile telephony in Asia Ewa Lechman. *Technological Substitution in Asia* (Routledge, 2017); Jeffrey James. 'Leapfrogging in Mobile Telephony.' *Technological Forecasting & Social Change* (Scribd, 2008).

9    'Mobile Cellular Subscriptions.' *World Bank Data.*

10   'ICTs Delivering Home-Grown Development Solutions in Africa.' *World Bank,* 2012.

11   A *'unique mobile subscriber'* is defined as an individual person that can account for multiple *'mobile connections'* (i.e. SIM cards). Most people in West Africa own more than one SIM card, i.e. subscribe to multiple mobile operators, for reasons which will be explored later in this study. 'The Mobile Economy, West Africa 2017.' *GSMA report, 2.*

12   As of December 2014, 89% of American adults owned a mobile phone, 'Cell Phones in Africa: Communication Lifeline.' *Pew Research Center's Global Attitudes Project,* 15 Apr. 2015.

# Chapter 2

## Consumer Appropriation:
## Case Study in Cameroon

### A. Introduction

In the context of mobile telephony, Africans appropriate the technology in that they explore a foreign object and choose how to integrate, or not integrate, it into their practices and daily lives (De Bruijn et al. 2009: 88). Professor of Communication François Bar argues that this engagement is deeply creative and fuels a powerful innovation engine (Bar 2010: 1). Bar distinguishes three phases in the appropriation process of mobile phones. First, adoption, refers to the use of mobile phones as envisioned by designers or mobile operators. In the second, appropriation, users experiment with mobile phones within limits pre-established by designers. The third phase, re-configuration, referred to as 'tropicalization' in this book, is a creative and subversive process driven by locals in reshaping mobile phones to make the technology their own. This categorization helps explain the process of consumer appropriation, but in this research I found that these three phases often overlap as the technology becomes embedded in the lives of users.

Through case studies in **Cameroon; Sudan; Tanzania; Burkina Faso; and Ghana,** anthropologists in *Mobile Phones: The New Talking Drums of Africa* demonstrate the societal changes brought by mobile telephony, as well as the ways in which mobile telephony has been reshaped under the influence of local creative usages and the process of becoming embedded in a cultural context. They argue that a thesis which presupposes Western tools and technology to be a colonizing force misses the point of appropriation and reduces the contradictory

25

meanings of technology to a simple homogenizing force. Mobile telephony cannot adhere to foreign schemes of 'colonization' or 'development' when it is appropriated in ways entirely unforeseen by its designers. Rather than interpreting the rise of mobile telephony as a victory of modernity over traditional African values, the following case study illustrates how Cameroonian ways of appropriating mobile phones have led to new practices, while simultaneously perpetuating and reshaping economic and social norms.

## B. Setting for the Field Research

Cameroon is a country situated along the Bight of Biafra, in the 'armpit' of Africa. In 1961, following independence, former French Cameroon and part of British Cameroon joined to form the United Republic of Cameroon. The country has been ruled by President Paul Biya for the past 36 years and is home to an estimated 25 million people.[13] While relatively stable and an important economic player in the region, Cameroon ranks 153rd on the Human Development Index.[14] To 'map' how the use of cell phones varies within Cameroon based on local realities, preliminary research for this study was conducted in the town of Bamenda (North-West region) and the village of Batoufam (Western region). The month-long field research took place in the rural district of Nyakokombo (Central region), the medium-size town of Buea (Southwest region), and the capital city Yaoundé (Central region).[15] The sample size of this research is 100 owners of mobile phones, 45 of which were surveyed in rural areas and the remaining 55 in urban areas. Participants answered surveys of 31 questions eliciting both qualitative and quantitative responses. Twenty-five surveys were collected from each of the following target groups: university students, civil servants, villagers, and members of the informal sector.[16]

To supplement this predominantly quantitative data and adequately study the appropriation of mobile telephony by the

Cameroonian population, 27 formal interviews were conducted with government officials, professors, students, call-box workers, a midwife, merchants, phone repairers, political activists, app developers, and regular citizens. This study does not account for the estimated 40% of the Cameroonian population under 15 years old, as the SIT program required all participants to be above 18 years old. However, 55% of participants surveyed lived in urban areas, which is closely representative of the country's estimated urban population of 54% in 2015.[17] Additionally, the percentage of males and females surveyed in this study are respectively 54% and 46%, which is close to the 49.9% of males and 50.1% of females who make up the overall population.[18] With no claim to be perfectly representative at the national level, trends perceived in this sample can nevertheless be assumed to be good illustrations of the appropriation of mobile telephony by the Cameroonian population.

The era of mobile telephony in Cameroon began in 1990, when the country collaborated with Siemens to become the first south of the Sahara with a Global System for Mobile Network (GSM) (Enyegue 2002: 23). Yet, communication costs remained exorbitant, penetration rates were low, and Cameroon, like most other West African nations, was undergoing a severe economic crisis. In the late 1990s, liberalization of the Cameroonian economy led the state to relinquish its monopoly on telecommunications and to license private telephone companies for the mobile sector. Presently, the two dominant mobile operators in Cameroon are Orange and MTN, combining for 94% of the telephone market shares in 2016.[19] Orange, a French owned telecommunication company, became the first private mobile telephony operator in Cameroon in 1999. Since its launch, Orange Cameroon has invested nearly 600 billion CFA ($1.122 billion), currently has 577 employees, out of which 99% are Cameroonian nationals, and controls around 37% of the telephone market.[20] In February 2000, Mobile

Telecommunication Network (MTN), a South-African owned company, launched its operations in Cameroon by acquiring the state-owned CamTel Mobile. MTN Cameroon is now the leading mobile operator in the country, holding 57% of telephone market shares in 2015. The company employs 1,000 people and is one of the most profitable companies in Cameroon. In the last fifteen years, MTN has invested over 2,200 billion CFA in Cameroon, close to US $4 billion, and over 80% of money generated from MTN operations are reinvested into the local economy.[21] MTN has also paid more than 800 billion CFA in taxes and duties, and its yearly fiscal contribution represents, on average, close to 3% of state revenue.

The other two mobile operators are Nexttel and Vodafone. Their shares of the market are still minimal as they only recently launched their operations in the country. In September 2014, Nexttel, co-owned by Vietnamese and Cameroonian investors, became the third private mobile telephony operator to enter the Cameroonian market. Nexttel was the first mobile operator in Cameroon to receive a 3G license, and by the end of 2015 the company already controlled 4.66% of the market.[22] In September 2016, Vodafone Cameroon was launched in the political and economic capitals, Yaoundé and Douala, which account for around 80% of the country's telecom market.[23] Vodafone is a British multinational mobile telephony operator, partnering in Cameroon with Afrimax, a 4G-LTE telecommunications operator in sub-Saharan Africa. At the time of this field research, Vodafone was still in the early implementation stages and had yet to provide mobile telephony services. As of early 2018, the company still lacked a license to operate in Cameroon. Thus, they were not considered for the purpose of this research.

With the advent of these private mobile operators and their partnerships with foreign companies, such as Huawei, Tecno Mobile, and Nokia, to produce cellphones, mobile penetration rates in Cameroon rose from almost nil to 80% in the span of fifteen years.[24] The privatization of the mobile telephony sector was a key step in the rapid expansion of the appropriation of mobile telephony from the elite to common people and in the 'glocalization' of the technology. However, despite the rise of private mobile operators between 2000 to 2015, the Cameroonian government has maintained jurisdiction over key sectors of the telecommunication market through its control of the Telecommunications Regulatory Agency (TRA) and CamTel. The government retains an important role in structuring the mobile economy and shaping certain forms of consumer appropriation.

The TRA is a public agency created in 1998 that serves as the right arm of the Ministry of Post and Telecommunications (MINPOSTEL) in regulating the Cameroonian telecommunication sector. For example, it oversees the 'Special Fund for Telecommunications', towards which mobile telephony operators must give 3% of their turnover.[25] The TRA is also meant to safeguard the principle of equal treatment of subscribers in all mobile telephony companies. It is granted executive powers by the state to sanction violations to laws concerning telecommunications, and as such it can be described as playing the role of referee between mobile telephony operators in Cameroon. CamTel is not only the lone state-owned mobile telephony operator in Cameroon, but also the sole landline telephony operator in the country. In 2015, however, CamTel held only 1.4% of telephone market shares, and to this day the company continues to encounter difficulties to supply landlines.[26] However, its importance in the mobile telephony market and in the appropriation of mobile telephony by consumers lies elsewhere.

CamTel simultaneously acts as a competitor and moderator for mobile telephony operators in Cameroon. The state-run company has a monopoly over the 'National Optical Fiber Backbone', meaning that it is in charge of laying out the infrastructure that will provide 'interconnection' between mobile telephony operators. Interconnection in the context of Cameroonian telecommunications means that CamTel oversees the process of allowing an operator, like MTN, to use the infrastructure or network of another operator, like Orange, in order for a call to go through. Communications between subscribers of different companies are more expensive than those within the same company. As such, Cameroonians check which company their contacts subscribe to by looking at the first few digits of their phone numbers. For example, the first digit of CamTel phone numbers is either '2' or '3'. Based on these numbers, Cameroonians know which SIM to use when calling their counterparts so they will not have to pay the price of interconnection. Subscribers own different SIMs, so they can change them based on the quality of the network in their location. Accordingly, most Cameroonians have multiple phone numbers and, for example, a different WhatsApp for each number which has often led me to receive the following response: 'Sorry for not responding earlier, but this number is not the one I use most for WhatsApp. I am more often connected with XXXX'. While mobile phones with dual-SIMs exist and SIMs are easily interchangeable, many prefer to own one phone per SIM. This is primarily a question of prestige and suggests that even if all networks were reliable, Cameroonians would most likely own multiple phones to show their social standing (De Bruijn et al. 2009: 5). Furthermore, the use of multiple SIMs explains why the rates of mobile subscriptions do not represent the number of people who own mobile phones in the country, but rather the number of SIMs activated amongst the overall population.

Keeping in mind that participants surveyed in this research often subscribe to multiple mobile companies, 66% of them subscribed to Orange, 63% subscribed to MTN, a surprising 41% subscribed to Nexttel, and 3% subscribed to CamTel. Despite being second in terms of subscribers in the sample, 40% of participants named MTN as their preferred operator, followed by Orange at 37% and Nexttel at 21% (the remaining 2% had no preference). When asked why they preferred a certain operator, 73% of participants said it was based on the quality of the network and services, 15% said it was a question of habit as they preferred the first operator they subscribed to, 7% said their preference was given to the mobile phone operator used by most of their contacts, and finally 5% did not answer or give a reason for their preference.

This overview of the methodology for the field research and of the Cameroonian telecommunications sector provides the necessary context for the question at the heart of this case study: how have Cameroonians taken ownership and appropriated the global technology of mobile telephony to fit their needs and local realities? The 'glocalization' of mobile telephony in Cameroon can be found in three main areas. The first way that Cameroonians have taken ownership of the *cellular economy*, is in the rise of an informal market for mobile phones and the evolution of mobile phone service as a result of the invention of the 'Call-Box system'. The second area is *consumptive appropriation,* i.e. the appropriation of mobile phones in ways which are directly or indirectly related to the consumption of goods and services, such as in the financial costs of owning a mobile phone and how the technology has helped reshape commerce. The third area is *creative appropriation,* or innovative forms of appropriation, as exemplified in the use of mobile phones by a traditional healer and the creation of mobile applications in response to local needs. These three aspects of mobile telephony in Cameroon illustrate how local agency can trump the neutrality of a means of communication in the process of 'appropriation'.

## C. The Informal Cellular Economy

The arrival of private mobile telephony operators in Cameroon brought an important opportunity for employment within the formal cellular economy. However, multinational telecommunication networks, like Orange and MTN, also implemented externalization strategies and subcontracted their services. This approach granted mobile operators flexibility to reduce the costs of their labor force and to transfer the cost of fluctuations in demand, but it did not lead to a significant increase in employment that the population had hoped for (Chéneau-Loquay 2010: 9). Instead, the subcontracting economy encouraged the appropriation of mobile telephony within the informal sector. The informal economy refers to various sectors operating outside of the government – regulated economy with unprotected labor relationships and not included in the Gross National Product (GNP) and Gross Domestic Product (GDP). However, grey areas and linkages exist between formal and informal activities. In this section the informal cellular economy is understood as economic activities which are not covered, but also those insufficiently covered by formal arrangements.[27]

In 2015, the International Labor Organization (ILO), a United Nations agency focused on labor issues, estimated that in developing countries the informal economy makes up half to three-quarters of non-agricultural employment (Raynor 2015: 16). In Cameroon, the International Monetary Fund (IMF) estimated in 2010 that the informal economy employs about 90% of the employed labor force – approximately 8 million people.[28] The informal cellular economy in Cameroon has led to the creation of what I call a cellphone trading and repairing empire, as well as the call-box system. This 'empire' in Cameroon is not limited to a certain geographical area. In the context of this study, however, it is primarily analyzed through observations and interviews conducted in Yaoundé and Bamenda, where mobile phone traders and repairers have appropriated this technology to jointly create a major sphere of 'glocalization'.

## a. The Trading and Repairing Empire

Avenue Kennedy is located in the heart of Yaoundé and is arguably the most prominent sector of mobile phone repairing and trading in Cameroon. The avenue swarms with street vendors who display mobile phones, mostly second-hand, on small tables or stands (see photo 1). Table sellers, known as 'vendeurs à la sauvette', and phone traders have set up shop in front of the headquarters of Orange and in close proximity to the other mobile operators. At first this appears to be disloyal competition, but active collaboration exists between mobile operators and street vendors. For example, when mobile operators offer a promotion on certain phones, street vendors are alerted so they can purchase them in bulk. Once the promotion ends, consumers turn to the 'vendeurs à la sauvette' who resell the mobile phones at a higher-price and give a percentage of these sales to the mobile operator. Cameroonians know to go to Avenue Kennedy if they want to sell their phone or trade an old phone and some cash for a new one. The table sellers are adamant that none of the mobile phones have been stolen, but they admit to having tricked customers into buying some that did not work. Either way they offer very attractive prices, selling working second-hand standard phones for 3,000 CFA ($5.40). For the sake of comparison, a large can of imported jam is sold at 3,700 CFA at the local supermarket.

Photo 1. Table sellers on Avenue Kennedy, Yaoundé

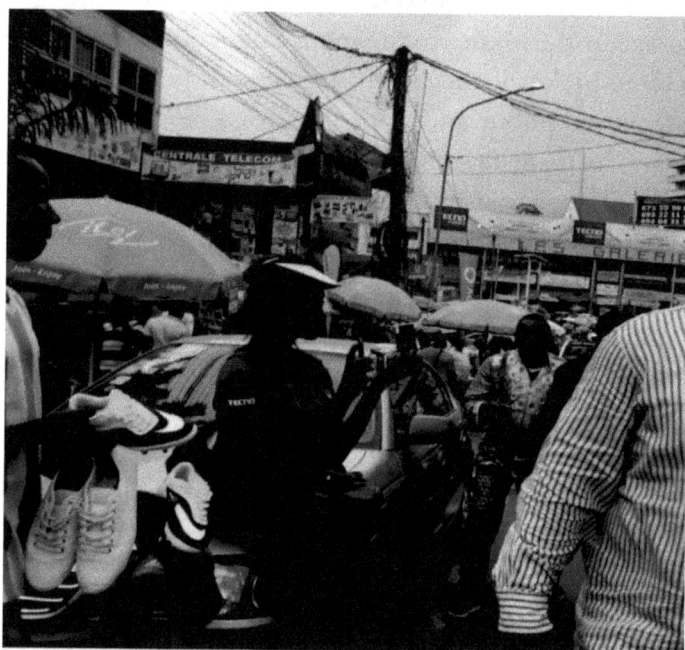

Photo 2. Young women selling phones on Avenue Kennedy

The street is also occupied by young women dressed in the uniforms of cellphone-producing companies like Nokia or Huawei (see photo 2). Not all customers feel comfortable venturing into the labyrinth of hallways that make up the buildings on Avenue Kennedy. Therefore, they can either buy a phone directly off one of these young ladies or ask to be directed to the shop that employs them. Many others try their luck and accost them in the hope of obtaining their personal numbers. Most wondering customers are approached by young men who welcome them with greetings along the lines of 'Tu cherches quoi mon frère?' ('What are you looking for my brother?'). Then depending on the needs of the customer, they will take them to a specific shop and usually the shop owner will give the young men between 50 CFA (a dime) and 150 CFA (a quarter) based on the value of the purchase made by the customer.[29] Mobile phone sellers with boutiques or spaces in these hallways are considered part of the informal cellular economy, but they still pay yearly taxes of up to 40,000 CFA ($72).

A man named 'Proxy' runs one of these cellphone shops on Avenue Kennedy (see photo 3). His makeshift boutique is made up of two shelves displaying cellphones and a few Apple tablets. Proxy is in his twenties and has the equivalent of an associate degree in commerce and marketing management studies. He is one of many young educated Cameroonians who entered the informal cellular economy to escape unemployment. Like many others Proxy is a 'bushfaller', meaning that he left his village for the city to 'hunt' in the hope of finding 'big game' (De Bruijn et al. 2009: 15). Even if they do not to return to their villages, 'bushfallers' face intense social pressure to share their acquired wealth with their rural kin.

To earn a living, Proxy works with some 'grand frères' ('big brothers') who travel to Dubai and bring back suitcases full of cheap Chinese manufactured mobile phones, and send what

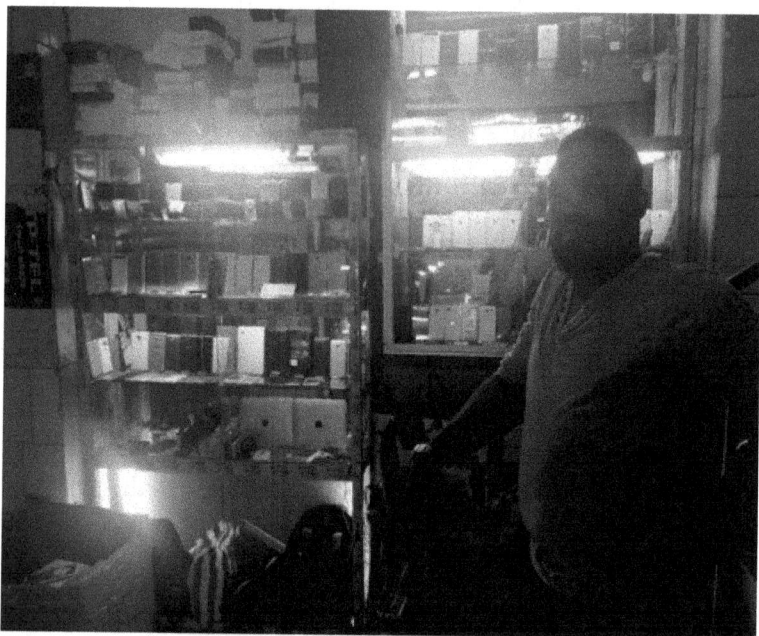

Photo 3. Proxy and his shop on Avenue Kennedy

they cannot carry via DHL packages. Proxy and other vendors are then in charge of selling these cellphones to the ordinary Cameroonian customer attracted by the low retail prices. Mobile phones are cheaper in such boutiques than at local mobile agencies, as sellers like Proxy do not have to abide by rigorous norms. A new Android can be purchased for around 15,000 CFA ($27), but it does not follow norms that would guarantee its quality.

The work of mobile phone traders like Proxy is not limited to the sale of low-cost mobile phones. They also provide internet configuration and app installation for MTN, Orange, and Nexttel subscribers. Once more, Proxy's services are cheaper and faster than at the telecom agencies where long waiting lines are the norm. Proxy's skills also extend to unlocking phones frozen due to pin code errors. If the pin code that comes with the SIM to unlock the phone is wrongly entered multiple times, the mobile phone locks and its user can no longer access it. This is common when mobile phones are stolen, but Proxy provides services with no questions asked. With their expansive skillset, people like Proxy blur the line between mobile phone trading and repairing. However, there are different degrees of mobile phone repairing, and certain phone repairers are renowned for being able to achieve the full 'tropicalization' of mobile phones.

Photo 4. Willy displaying second-hand batteries he will fix to be reused

Willy is a phone repairer with a shop on Commercial Avenue, the equivalent in Bamenda of Avenue Kennedy (see photo 4). On top of his small store he installed a solar panel that provides current for all his electrical outputs. Just like most phone repairers in Cameroon (Nkwi 2015: 10), Willy is equipped with a Power Station that helps remove Integrated Circuits (ICs). The presence of heat is necessary to remove ICs without creating a short circuit. Power stations not only provide this heat but also detect variations in the temperature of the mobile phone while it is being repaired. Willy knows the temperature at which the mobile phone can be operated on without overheating. Once the ICs are properly removed, Willy proceeds to work on it and if needed can alter a foreign phone display to a Cameroonian display.

Willy claims to be self-taught – like the majority of phone repairers in Cameroon – and to have learned his skills on the internet, YouTube or by watching others at work. For lack of better options, Cameroonians like Willy have entered the world of phone repairers and are now able to 'tropicalize' mobile phones. Proxy defines the process of tropicalization as 'adapting a foreign network to the tropical zone, so we "Cameroonize" the cellphone in order to be connected'.[30] This 'Cameroonization' of mobile phones includes installing software to transform a 'purely French' SFR phone so that it can function with local mobile telephony operators. Repairers use a modem to have constant internet access on their laptops and, in turn, are able to download software. In this case, software is used so the SFR mobile phone can recognize the Cameroonian SIM card and have access to services such as mobile money. Then 'configuration codes, algorithms, updates, re-programming and other parameters', are installed to finalize the transition of a 'French phone' to a 'Cameroonian phone'. Technological appropriation and 'tropicalization' of the mobile phone is achieved.

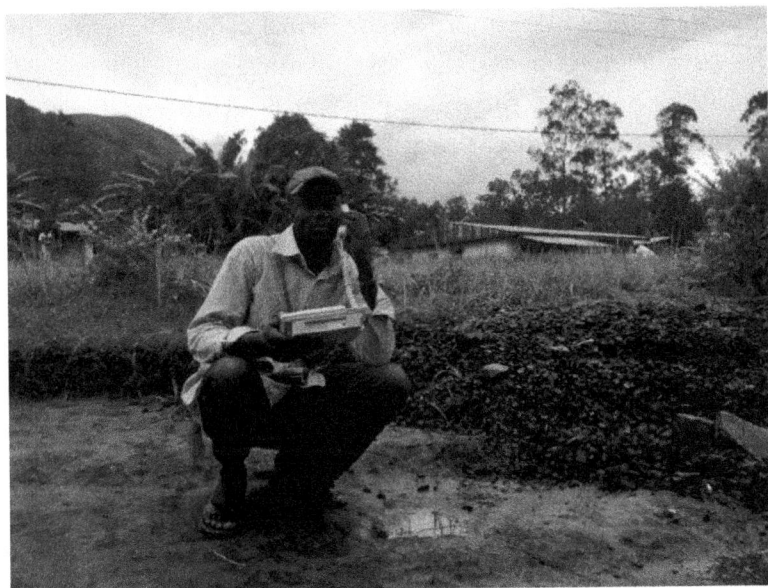

Photo 5. The villager in Big Babanki holding his 'mobile-landline' phone

A man in Big Babanki, a village near Bamenda, exemplifies the notion of cellular 'tropicalization' as he walks around talking on a wireless landline-type phone (see photo 5). His friend had brought back this 'mobile-landline' phone as a gift from his travels in Japan and it has been locally reconfigured to integrate a Cameroonian SIM card and to send text messages like a regular mobile phone. To prevent his wife from looking through his contacts, the villager entered over 200 anonymous numbers in his phone. To remember which number belonged to which contact, he memorized the last 3 digits of each one. This man illustrates how local agency operating within the sphere of 'glocalization' and the local informal cellular economy, leads to the appropriation of the technology. The informal economy in Cameroon is a major sphere of 'glocalization', as mobile phones from abroad are tailored to increasingly distinguishable local and particular markets. By operating outside of corporate structures and creating a bilateral mobile economy, Cameroonians like

Proxy and Willy are able to achieve this technological appropriation. Furthermore, the informal cellular economy has the advantage of being largely self-sufficient: the cheaper the mobile phones are, the more they break down and the more frequently they need repairing. If repairing is not enough, then a new phone is bought, which perpetuates the cycle and ensures the durability of the mobile phone trading and repairing empire.

### b. The Call-Box System

For the majority of users in Cameroon, cell phone service runs on a per-minute credit system rather than a monthly plan. The call-box system is a process by which Cameroonians can borrow the cellphone of a call-boxer to make calls at a lower per-minute tariff than if using their own mobile phone. The call-box itself is usually about 60x60 cm and 190 cm high (Nkwi 2014: 6), made of timber with plywood on the lower half and with four windows that open outwards (see photo 6). The customer pays the call-boxer for the amount of credit he desires, then credit is transferred to his phone. 'Super Dealers', i.e. an agent or company, organize the dissemination of call-credit from the mobile telephony operator to the population. Call-boxers do not deal directly with 'Super-Dealers' but rather with suppliers who are assigned certain neighborhoods where they deliver credit to call-boxers.

In major cities, most call-boxers call their suppliers in the morning and ask for a certain amount of credit for the day. The supplier then sends them credit through their mobile phone and in the evening will come collect the money owed. In 2014, close to 99% of MTN, Orange, and Nexttel subscribers operated on pre-paid calling services, i.e. pay-as-you go formula, like the ones offered by the call-box.[31]

In the rural district of Nyakokombo, call-boxers are asked to give the money first before a supplier will send the credit by phone (see photo 7). As such, a couple of times a week call-boxers will give money to a trusted motorcycle-taxi man, the bread deliverer in one case, who will then bring it to the mobile phone operator's agency in town.[32] Once the call-boxer has acquired credit, it is stored in his phone(s) and can be distributed to the general public using EVD (Electronic Voucher Distribution).[33] The customer tells the call-boxer how much he wants and the call-boxer goes into *services, credit transfer,* then *sale* and hands the phone over to the customer so he can enter his phone number. A few seconds later, the customer should receive a message confirming the success of the transaction.

Photo 6. A typical call-box in Buea, Cameroon (2007)

Photo 7. Call-boxer in Nyakokombo

A wide range of people in urban and rural areas benefit from the call-box system today, but its creation was primarily rooted in the agency of Cameroonian women. The economic crisis starting in the mid-1980s left many Cameroonians unemployed, and most households had to come up with creative ways to make ends meet. At the turn of the century, many Cameroonian women responded to the rapid spread of mobile phones by creating call-boxes where users could make calls and transfer credit. In the early 2000s, the call-box system was lucrative as mobile phones were reserved for the elite and calling rates were much higher than they are today. In 2009, eight years after the arrival of mobile phones in Buea, this city of approximately 90,000 people was home to at least 550 call-boxes (Nkwi 2009: 57). Out of 200 call-box workers surveyed and interviewed during his research in Buea, Professor Walter Gam Nkwi tallied 150 women. Thanks to their appropriation of the call-box system, many of these women were able to pay school fees for themselves or their children, attain better medical services, provide revenue to the state by paying yearly taxes and overall achieve greater sustainability through self-employment (Nkwi 2014: 10). The call-box system back then could thus be described as a well-regulated appropriation of mobile telephony's call services by Cameroonians.[34] As time went on, however, local realities changed and so did the appropriation of the call-box system.

Nowadays the call-box business is less lucrative as it is scarcely used to make calls, due to the spread of mobile phones and attractive bonuses offered by operators. Calls emitted from the call-box can cost either 25 CFA or 50 CFA for the first 59 seconds. As soon as the customer goes over the 59 second threshold, then 25 CFA or 50 CFA are automatically added to his bill. This little 'trick' allowed call-boxers to earn most of their money thanks to calls, but now customers primarily come for credit transfers. Despite the rise of mobile banking, which allows subscribers to convert money in a mobile account into call-credit, the call-box is still widely used to purchase credit. In this study, 77% of the participants claimed that it is their preferred way of buying credit, while 22% chose mobile banking. Call-boxers, however, only earn about 5% of the credit they sell.[35] This means that for 10,000 CFA ($18) worth of credit sold, the call-boxer makes a small profit of 500 to 600 CFA ($1).

Call-boxers have adapted to downfalls in cellular revenue by selling other small products. These include bita cola nuts, tissues, soft drinks, fruits, cigarettes, and illegal whisky sachets.[36] Many call-boxers earn most of their profit by selling these small products. One call-boxer interviewed for this study earned more from selling whisky and cigarettes than from selling call-credit (see photo 8). The net profit of 1,600 CFA she makes from selling whisky is equivalent to what she would earn if she sold 30,000 CFA worth of credit. Furthermore, most call-boxes in urban cities like Yaoundé are no longer made of actual wooden boxes but rather involve a call-boxer sitting under an umbrella provided by mobile telephony operators. Others now roam the streets with their umbrella in hand and have effectively become 'a human call-box'. By constantly moving, these ambulant call-boxers evade taxes while those who sit under their umbrella run away with their products when they see employees of the local council. Accordingly, the call-box system has transitioned from an actual wooden box used by women to empower themselves within a well-regulated system to a non-regulated mobile phone shop.[37] Competition between call-boxers increased as the demand for their services decreased, leaving them to re-appropriate the call-box system in a different way to fit their needs and local realities.

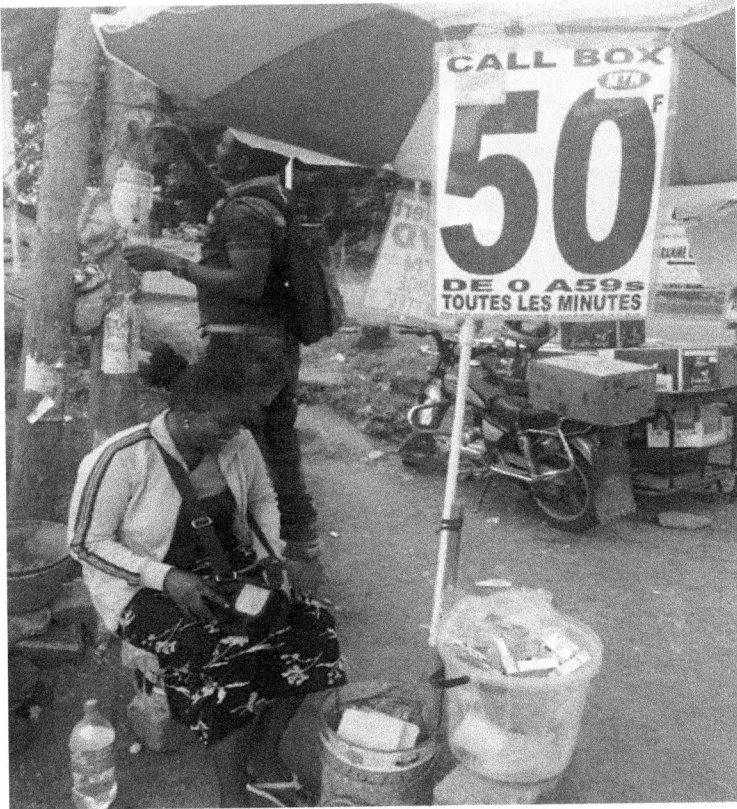

Photo 8. Call-boxer in Yaoundé selling a wide range of products

## D. Consumptive Appropriation

Consumptive appropriation is an umbrella term understood in this study as the financial and societal costs of mobile phones incurred on subscribers in the process of adopting mobile phones. While the informal economy often leads to technological forms of re-configuration, consumptive forms of appropriation account for the financial costs of mobile phones for their most basic usages and their adoption with regards to local realities. The ICT4D discourse brings light to the income-generating uses of mobile phones, such as increasing the efficiency of commercial transactions, yet there are also important financial costs related to the adoption of mobile phones. The financial burden of mobile phones on consumers includes its price of purchase, maintenance and services. However, the appropriation of mobile phones by Cameroonians is not limited to financial costs, as it has also led to societal costs which include distraction for the youth, theft, and relationship troubles. The societal costs of mobile phones and constant connection have been widely documented, most recently by Vivek Wadhwa and Alex Salkever who delve into the impact of technology on human interactions and psyche in their work titled *Your Happiness Was Hacked* (2018). Through the spread of mobile phones, this reality of omnipresent technology is increasingly found in West Africa and has led to distinct societal costs. Through an analysis of the financial and societal costs of mobile phones, as well as the reforms brought to the commercial sector, this sub-section analyzes how local agency has created a 'consumptive' form of mobile telephony appropriation in Cameroon.

### a. *The Financial and Societal Costs of Owning a Mobile Phone*

The monthly minimum wage in Cameroon stands at 36,270 CFA ($65).[38] Thirty-eight percent of participants surveyed in this study had a monthly revenue well below this minimum wage, as it ranged between 0-20,000CFA, and 9% identified the financial burden of mobile phones as the main problem linked to the technology (see Figure 2).

## Range of Monthly Revenue in CFA

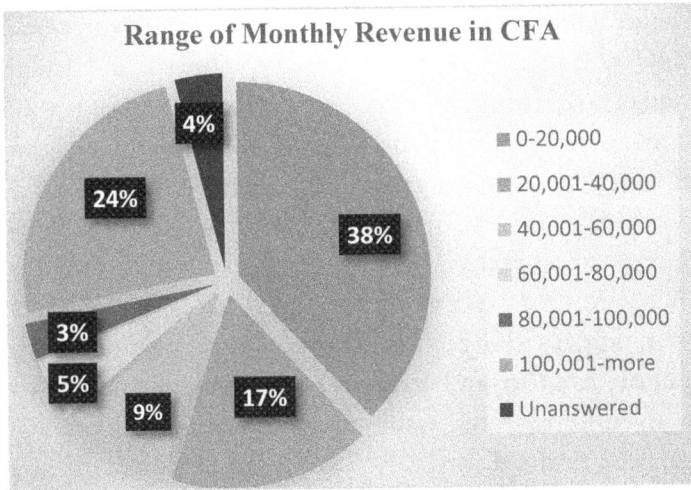

Figure 2. Range of Monthly Revenue in CFA

Yet, the financial difficulties of participants did not prevent them from owning mobile phones. A total of 138 mobile phones were owned by 100 participants, with 92% of phones costing from 0 to 100,000 CFA ($181).[39] Despite the fact that only 3% of the population surveyed earned between 80,001-100,000 CFA a month, 11% of participants were able to purchase mobile phones at prices above 80,000 CFA and many others were willing to spend a month worth of earnings to make the purchase. Part of the explanation stems from the aforementioned social standing associated with cellphone ownership and the need to be included in what President Paul Biya called 'the Android generation'.[40] Mobile phones have become synonymous with 'good', and are embedded as such in the local lingo, as many Cameroonians like to refer to 'Android girls' or even 'Android meat skewers'. Financial spending on phones, however, is not limited to the purchase of the device.

Mobile phone owners must buy credit to make calls, send messages, and have internet data (if the standard of their phone permits it). On a weekly basis, 45% of participants spent more than 100 CFA on credit and those with smartphones also incur high costs for internet data in a country ranked 40th in the world out of 46 countries on the internet Affordability Index (Nyamnjoh et al. 2016: 87). Furthermore, once the mobile phone is purchased, 85% of participants go on to buy a memory card. The cost of these memory cards ranges between 2,500 CFA ($4.50) for 4 gigabytes (GB) and 42,400 CFA ($76.75) for 64 GB.[41] The cost and need for memory cards explain why 12% of participants identified greater memory space, along with greater battery duration, as the main improvement needed for their mobile phone. Apart from battery duration, charging cellphone batteries is an important issue in rural areas deprived of electricity, such as the district of Nyakokombo. Along with not being able to use their mobile phone, consumers incur financial losses as bonuses can expire while the mobile phone is off. Improving battery duration is difficult at the level of villagers in Nyakokombo, but the lack of electricity called upon their creativity to charge their mobile phones.

In order to charge their mobile phones, most inhabitants of Nyakokombo own a small portable solar panel (see photo 9). These solar panels are bought for around 17,000 CFA ($30). The use of solar panels to charge mobile phones is common throughout sub-Saharan Africa and has led to innovations particularly useful in rural areas deprived of electricity. In Rwanda, entrepreneur Henry Nyakarundi created a solar-powered kiosk that can be towed by bicycle and provide simultaneous charging for up to 80 phones.[42] However, solar-powered kiosks are still uncommon and in Nyakokombo, like most villages, the norm is for villagers to place the solar panels on top of their roofs and connect them to their phones using a USB cord. If they lack a USB cord then they put the wires 'en direct', meaning that using rubber bands they attach the positive and negative wires to the corresponding poles on the battery.[43] If the polarization is not respected, then the mobile phone will short circuit. Those who do not use solar panels can charge their phones using a generator, in addition to its original price the generator needs three liters of gas to function, each liter costing around 800 CFA. As such, these rural inhabitants found a third innovative way to charge their mobile phones, using the generator located at the local Orange antenna. Villagers give 200 CFA to the Orange security guard at the antenna to charge and guard their mobiles phones. Around three hours later they come back to pick it up. The services provided by the security guard are not included in his contract, but as villagers rationalize, 'the goat grazes where it is attached'. Taking into consideration the purchase of the phone, credit, a memory card, and a solar panel, in the first year of owning a mobile phone an inhabitant of Nyakokombo earning the national minimum wage will allocate around 12% of his yearly revenue on mobile telephony.[44] Along with financially burdening forms of consumptive appropriation, the appropriation of mobile phone translates into important societal costs.

Photo 9. A villager in Nyakokombo charging her
phone using a solar panel

The three primary societal costs of mobile phones observed during this research are: distraction among the youth, strained relationships, and cellular criminality. Twenty percent of participants acknowledged the distraction and dependence engendered by mobile phones as one of the main problems linked to the technology. Paradoxically, 36% of participants stated that they could not do without mobiles phones, as they are required for their work or studies. In Nyakokombo, mobile phones are not allowed in classrooms because students often access pornographic websites during class time or play music instead of using them to study.[45] Similarly in New York City, from 2006 to 2015, mobile phones were not seen as conducive to learning and were legally prohibited in schools to reduce distraction and cheating. As a result, 'phone trucks' appeared in front of high schools where for $1 students could leave their phone for the day.[46] Yet, the application of the law varied depending on the institution and was amended, leaving it up for the schools to decide. The debate in the United States, a country where in 2000 camps for 'digital detox' were invented, is far from having come to a close. Likewise, in 2018, phones were banned from schools in France - even during recess to encourage interpersonal rapport. Mobile phones can be detrimental to educational practices, from Nyakokombo to New York, and while they are a communication technology they tend to decrease face-to-face interactions.

Mobile phones can also negatively affect romantic relationships. In 2016, a prominent Cameroonian music artist known as 'Franko' released a single called 'Telephone'. The song has been viewed over 2.4 million times on YouTube, and the chorus is as follows:

'Ooorrr ma chérie écoute
Le téléphone est devenu un véritable danger pour les couples
Téléphone a gâté les mariages
Téléphone a gâté les foyers

50

Téléphone a semé les bagarres
Pardon celui de ton gars, faut pas toucher'[47]

The participants surveyed in this study confirmed Franko's assessment of how mobile phones can impact relationships, as 22% percent of them identified 'relationship issues' as the main problem linked to mobile phones. Yet, it appears that the trouble at hand is not the mobile phone itself but how it facilitates and brings to light the problem of infidelity – posing the question of the neutrality of the technology which I address in Chapter 4. The most common example cited by participants was when one of their lovers calls them in the presence of their official partner or simply when their significant other scours through their phone. This might explain why 41% of participants have installed security codes on their mobile phones. However, these trust issues can sometimes result in drastic measures. One participant acknowledged that before travelling he puts all of his wife's contacts into a 'black-list'. As such, she can only call and receive calls from her husband. Unintentionally, her husband might also be protecting her from 'cellular criminals'.

When mobile phones first arrived, thefts of these prized items were rampant. Despite the democratization of mobile phones, thefts are still common, as 60% of the participants in this study claim to have had their mobile phone stolen at least once. This phenomenon is not unique to West Africa, in fact in major U.S. cities roughly 50% of all robberies involve the theft of mobile devices.[48] Yet, carriers in many countries still choose not to share data on phone thefts beyond their own borders, allowing thieves to trade these stolen devices around the world in an underground network now believed to be worth $30 billion a year. The vast majority of stolen smartphones from the U.S. are sent to Hong Kong where they are 'unlocked, re-flashed, re-kitted' – meaning that they are put in a new box, with new accessories and an instruction manual in the language of the country of destination. West Africa and its bustling centers of the informal cellular economy, such as 'Avenue Kennedy' but most importantly 'Tiptoe Lane' in Ghana, are some of the prime destinations for this second-hand market.[49] While this trade of pilfered devices is often advantageous to Cameroonians looking to purchase mobile phones at low-cost, the culture of cellular theft is also prominent locally, and mobile phones are also used as tools to orchestrate larger criminal activities.

One participant recounted a time when, supposedly, villagers alerted thieves in Yaoundé that she would be traveling to the capital. Upon her arrival they jumped her. In cases like these, mobile phones can be stolen, but the thieves primarily use them to obtain other goods. Other times, the thefts are not physical but occur through the phone. For example, the president of an association in Nyakokombo once received a call from someone introducing himself as a local prefect. The interlocutor said he was arriving in Nyakokombo with some guests but that his car was stuck in the mud on the bad roads leading up to the district. Due to her position as the president of the local association, he asked her to transfer 6,000 CFA so he could re-fill his credit and call for assistance. The so-called prefect never showed up and the money evaporated. Such acts have become common and are referred to as 'scamming'.[50] Scamming is the act of using mobile phones, internet and such to extort money, often targeting people in the West. Nonetheless, in Yaoundé a taxi driver once drove across the city to return my phone which had slipped out of my pocket in the crowded backseat. The passengers and taxi-man may have been the exception to the rule but a notable one. In all, along with financial costs directly and indirectly related to the purchase, maintenance and services of mobile phones there are also societal costs. Societal costs occur as the consumption of goods and services related to mobile phones have become a form of distraction, enhanced relationship issues and lead to cellular criminal activities.

## b. *Reforming Commerce*

Although mobile phone ownership comes at significant costs, there are also benefits in the consumptive appropriation of mobile telephony by Cameroonians. These advantages are largely realized in the field of commerce. The rise of mobile money and the use of mobile phones to call commercial partners have helped facilitate and reform the commercial sector. In 2014, 34% of African adults had a mobile money account while only 2% of adults worldwide used this service.[51] In 2015, out of the 411 million accounts existing around the world, more than half were found in sub-Saharan Africa, where only 34% of adults had a bank account in 2014.[52] Accordingly, sub-Saharan Africa is the epicenter of global mobile money services.

Mobile money services in Cameroon have been available since September 2011 and are offered by Orange, with 'Orange Money', and by MTN, with 'Mobile Money'. Mobile money refers to the process of transfering money through mobile phones and can be described as an electronic wallet which allows for the convenient transfer of funds.[53] Commercial banks have partnered with mobile phone operators to provide regulatory supervision in the usage of this electronic wallet. In 2015, over 700 payment locations were available across Cameroon where customers could deposit or withdraw money transferred through mobile banking.[54] Unlike most banks, mobile money does not require a minimum balance requirement and any amount of money can be cashed in or out.

Mobile money's availability and ease of use are the principal attractions for its customers. Transferring currency from a mobile money account to turn it into call-credit is one option available which is particularly popular. In this study, 22% of participants identified it as their preferred way of transferring credit. In a country where only a minority has a bank account, like most sub-Saharan African nations, mobile banking is used in lieu of credit cards and allows subscribers to pay their electricity, internet, water bills, cable subscriptions, university tuition, and even taxes without having to visit an office or wait in line.[55] Four years after its launch, mobile money had already been adopted by 25% of mobile phone users in Cameroon.[56] Despite mobile money's early success and growing popularity, a large portion of the population – especially in rural areas – still uses other ways to conduct its commercial activities.

In the district of Nyakokombo, the main commercial activities have long been the sale of fish, cocoa and parrots. Before the arrival of mobile phones, cocoa farmers had to listen closely to the national radio in order to know the market prices for their goods or simply accept the prices offered by buyers. Nowadays, these farmers can use their mobile phones to follow variations in market prices as frequently as needed. Rather than having to surf the internet or download applications, they simply call contacts who inform them of the market prices in London. By knowing the prices in London and in Douala, they can find the appropriate retail price based on local realities. For example, if one kilo of cocoa is sold in Douala for 1,500 CFA ($2.71) then farmers in Nyakokombo sell one kilo of cocoa for around 1,250 CFA ($2.26). This drop in price accounts for the bad roads representatives of cocoa companies will take to reach Nyakokombo and the lack of a warehouse for all the cocoa harvested by the different farmers in the village, which prevents representatives from collecting all the cocoa at once. Once the cocoa is ready to be sold, the farmers can now call the representatives of cocoa companies and all the delegates from surrounding villages to meet and negotiate sale prices.

Farmers in countries like Niger, Senegal and Ghana can now also type in a code, send a text message, and receive the price of a variety of goods instantaneously (Aker and Mbiti 2010: 207-232). Over 200,000 farmers across ten different countries in West Africa use the 'Farmerline' application to receive weather updates, updated markets prices, and advice in local languages.[57] Many of these farmers have seen their profits increase by 50% since they've started using the app. In Burkina Faso, where shea butter is one of the main exports, farmers use mobile phones and global positioning systems to track 'locations, surface area, number of trees and other data' to harvest shea butter and sell it over the internet. Mobile phones are also enhancing the reach of agricultural extension services, such as in Kenya and Uganda where farmers can call or text hotlines to ask for technical agricultural advice. Such practices are also common in other regions of the world, including in India, and unlike the 'Farmerline' application they do not necessitate smartphones. Considering that Africa's population is projected to surpass 2 billion people by 2050, farm productivity must accelerate at a faster rate than the global average to avoid food deprivation. While it is still too early to evaluate the impact of the digitalization of farming in Africa, mobile phones are increasingly improving productivity and human welfare in the agricultural sector, which accounts for more than 30% of the continent's GDP and employs more than 60% of its working population.[58]

In a recent past, tam-tams were used to communicate across neighboring villages and bring together inhabitants, hence the *Talking Drums of Africa* by John Carrington, with different rhythms signaling specific messages. Now thanks to mobile phones, organizing inter-village meetings has become easier and farmers are less likely to be tricked into selling their cocoa below market prices. Similarly, parrot capturers and fishermen use their mobile phones to alert their commercial partners. Previously buyers would ask for a number of parrots to be captured by a certain deadline. On that date, the buyer would travel to Nyakokombo and at times find that not enough parrots had been collected. Now the capturers simply call the buyer when their order is ready (see photo 10). These grey parrots with red hearts are often purchased by middlemen for 12,000 CFA ($21) and then sent to South Africa – the hub of the parrot trade – before being transported by plane to Europe and the Middle East where they are on average purchased for 600,000 CFA

($1,000). African grey parrots are the most coveted species of parrots in the world, as they are the best talker of them all. Over the past four decades 1.3 million greys have been legally exported from West and Central African countries, but in 2016 they were placed on the list of species threatened with extinction and must now be raised in captivity in order to be sold abroad.[59] Fishermen in Nyakokombo also indulge in an expansive regional trade network facilitated by the advent of mobile phones. Fishermen can sell cooking pots full of fish for 100,000 CFA ($181), which are then taken to Gabon, Nigeria and Equatorial Guinea to be sold once more. The advent of a modern service like mobile money has progressively reformed certain aspects of the commercial sector, yet as shown in the case of cocoa farmers, parrot capturers and fishermen in Nyakokombo, the mobile phone's most basic utility, i.e. calling, has also helped facilitate commerce for merchants.

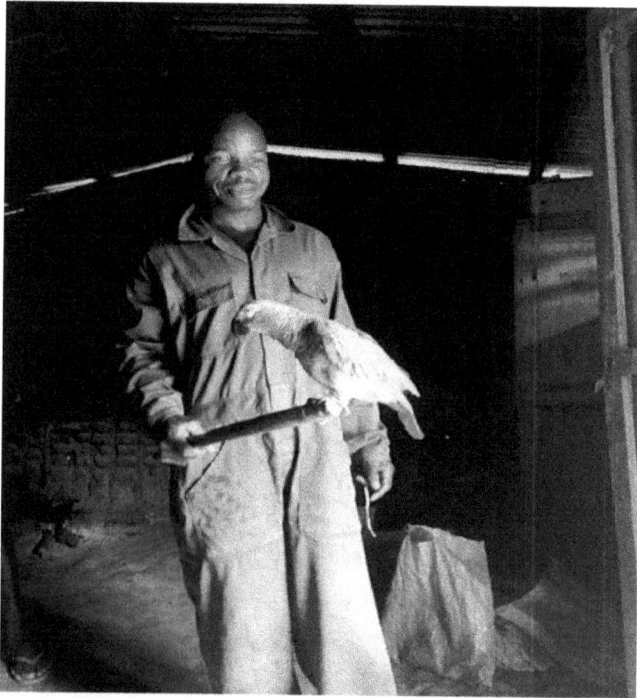

Photo 10. Parrot hunter in Nyakokombo

# E. Creative Appropriation

Creative forms of appropriation display ways in which mobile phones are used in particularly innovative forms of adaptation to local needs. This includes the rise of start-ups developing mobile applications and the College of Technology in Buea. Such centers of mobile innovation have received extensive media coverage, including at the international level, and are primarily driven by the desire of the youth to create digital solutions to local shortcomings. Yet, contrasting with the notion that modern technologies supersede traditional ways to bring about modernity, this study finds that creative forms of mobile appropriation often bring change in continuity rather than groundbreaking transformations. Mobile innovations often serve to uphold traditional ways of life, while simultaneously re-shaping them. As explained by Cameroonian scholar David Simo, such initiatives are 'neither a reflex of conservation at all costs, nor a retreat into something sacred and untouchable, but the re-appropriation of the initiative, the creation of a new endogenous dynamic to face the challenges of a globalizing world' (Simo 1998: 139). To illustrate the creative appropriations at the heart of this endogenous dynamic, this subsection draws on the use of mobile phones by a traditional healer in the village of Batoufam and the mobile applications invented by young entrepreneurs in the 'Silicon Mountain' of Buea.

## a. Resourcefulness in Societal Adaptations

The 'tradi-practitioner' – or traditional healer – had drawn a circle on the ground with chalk and bordered it with fetishes and totems. Three wooden sticks were held together by string in the form of a triangle, and an elderly woman was standing in the middle of the circle. She was holding a mirror on which rested pictures of her relatives, whom the tradi-practitioner was meant to heal. As he was reciting incantations, a ringtone went off. The tradi-practitioner reached in his pocket, pulled out a small standard phone and answered the call. Then he walked away from his patient to carry on with his cellular conversation, interrupting the ceremony and leaving her standing with the mirror in hand (see photo 11).

Photo 11. Tradi-practitioner in Batoufam, answering a call during a 'distance healing' ceremony

He later clarified that the call was from another patient and that patients commonly call for his services. He also explained that the ceremony being conducted was meant to 'heal at a distance' – meaning that none of the patients were present but their grandmother wanted the tradi-practitioner to cast away bad spirits from them. Distance healing is still commonly practiced in Cameroon, and the mobile phone has been appropriated to help facilitate the process.

Mobile phones have greatly facilitated the work of tradi-practitioners, as patients can now call to describe their illness or trouble. The tradi-practitioners then performs his diagnoses, prescribes his medication, and negotiates financial transactions over the phone. Tradi-practitioners do not limit their expertise to healing relatives at a distance or curing patients suffering from malaria or dysentery. They also provide medication to pass exams, to achieve success at work, or to get revenge on one's enemies (Van Beek 2009: 129). Once the tradi-practitioner receives the money, he uses it to send the products to his patient's post-office box. The patient collects the packages and calls the tradi-practitioner, who tells him how and when the medicine must be taken. This process is especially effective as 'one must believe in order to heal' and surrender entirely to the healer.[60] Additionally, when patients are healed their disease is believed to disperse, meaning that it could possibly 'contaminate' the tradi-practitioner if he were to be in the presence of the patient. Mobile phones are a remedy to this issue, as the distance between the healer and his patient is safeguarded. Tradi-practitioners now use this technology to reach and treat patients over a far wider geographic range than was previously possible. The network of patients of some tradi-practitioner even spreads to Europe, where expatriated Cameroonians solicit their services. Mobile phones have thus been appropriated to bring change in continuity in the field of traditional healing.

Creativity in the use of mobile phones has also reached the political field. In 2014, 100 million Africans were using Facebook each month, and over 80% of them accessed it through their mobile phone.[61] In 2015, the number of Facebook users in Africa reached 120 million. In Cameroon, in 2017 there were a little over 6.1 million internet users, out of an estimated 24.5 million people, and 2.1 million of these internet users had a Facebook account.[62] Accordingly, a third of Cameroonians who have access to the internet subscribe to Facebook. In this study, 47% of participants using applications listed Facebook as one of their favorites, while 72% of participants favored the number one free-messaging app in the world, WhatsApp.[63] Such social media and communication applications are primarily used to communicate and follow the news.[64] Overall, 28% of participants surveyed are members of WhatsApp, Facebook or other groups of more than 100 people. Sixty-four percent of these groups are related to work or educational purposes and 50% related to social or family affairs. One of the major appropriations of such Facebook and WhatsApp groups by Cameroonians is for political purposes. For example, 'Le Cameroun C'est Le Cameroun' (LCCLC), is a popular Facebook group created in 2010 which gained 172,000 members in the span of eight years.[65] In a single day its administrators often receive around 650 requests for admission from Facebook users. The members of the group must abide to a chart, i.e. a constitution, which serves to regulate what can and cannot be said in the hope of reducing posts that are considered to be 'out of line'. Such social media groups often escape media censure, and to the dislike of government officials they are now considered to be 'the manifestation of citizen expression'.[66] For example, in 2016, LCCLC brought to light the 'Koumate case' by organizing a march in support of a pregnant women who died in gruesome fashion on the doorstep of a hospital in Douala as she could not afford medical services.[67] Likewise, in 2016 following the Eseka train derailment which killed 70 passengers, videos of the victims were shared on LCCLC contradicting initial reports of government officials denying any fatalities.

As highlighted in the case of the Arab Spring, WhatsApp groups and social media also facilitate the organization of social manifestations and popular uprisings, acting both as a rallying cry and a megaphone spreading information across regions and national borders.[68] In the Anglophone region of Cameroon, mobile communication outlets have fueled significant protests which have led the national government to shutdown internet access in the Southwest and Northwest province.[69] Most LCCLC administrators are members of the Cameroon Renaissance Movement (MRC), a prominent opposition party in Cameroon, and use the platform to advance their political agenda. Nonetheless, the engagements of groups like LCCLC outside of the cyberspace are limited and they have yet to upend the Cameroonian political landscape. Critics of LCCLC argue that at its origin the group had a good reason to exist, but due to the partisan aspect of its administrators it fell victim to invectives and has become more of a playful group where people can release pent-up feelings and spread fake news.[70]

Through a creative political appropriation of Facebook, primarily accessed by mobile phone, cyber-activists with a pro-change ideology are able to form virtual political parties. This appropriation is a financially inexpensive way to create a powerful movement that can counteract state media propaganda and unite Cameroonians with common views, without the fear of being censured. Such social media groups, however, have been condemned for propagating fake news and enhancing the culture of gossip and rumor mongering known as 'radio trottoir' in West Africa (Ellis 1989: 321-330). In January 2017, the Cameroonian Minister of Posts and Telecommunications, Libom Li Likeng, announced the start of a sensibilisation campaign against fake news.[71] Since then, Cameroonians regularly receive messages on WhatsApp or Facebook reminding them that the spread of fake news is a crime punishable by up to 3 years in prison and a fine of 2 million CFA ($3,620). Grassroots activism and the creative political appropriation of social media through mobile phones has offered a new form of political opposition while also enhancing the spread of misinformation in Cameroonian society.

## b. Local Realities and App Development in the 'Silicon Mountain'

The Director of the College of Technology of the University of Buea (UB) hopes that graduates of the college will be able 'to provide solutions to the local needs' and 'have self-sustainable employment'.[72] In order to achieve these goals, the college has a computer engineering department as well as an electrical and electronic engineering department, which teach coding for app development and website designs (see photo 12). In the class 'Mobile Application: Using Android', students code applications on computers and then connect their Android to them, in order to directly test the applications.[73] Thanks to this combination of computers and mobile phones, students were able to create the online platform for the University of Buea, an app which gives its user an estimate of the power that his electronics at home are consuming, and another app which allows for calls within the campus network to be free of charge.[74] With the skills mastered at the College of Technology, students often go on to work for mobile phone operators or create their own start-ups.[75] These students are the main reasons why Buea has been referred to as the 'Silicon Mountain' or the 'Silicon Valley of Cameroon'.[76]

Photo 12. 'Internet Application Programming' course at the College of Technology in Buea

Photo 13. App developers at the first annual gathering of
ActivSpaces in Buea

The offices of ActivSpaces, the best-known start-up in the
region, are a five-minute taxi ride away from the University of
Buea. ActivSpaces employs ten people and serves as an
incubator for young entrepreneurs looking for an adequate
working environment to create their applications. The
company's success in creating applications has been recognized
internationally in news coverage by BBC Afrique and France 24.
Most ActivSpaces members are UB students working on various
applications, such as an app that would assist fellow students in
scheduling their classes by automatically generating a timetable
with their courses.[77] In November 2016, as part of 'Global
Entrepreneurship Week', ActivSpaces hosted its first
countrywide gathering of app developers (see photo 13). The
array of applications available on mobile phones presented
included 'Speed Kart', a grocery delivery service; 'Checkche',
which puts people who lost their ID card in touch with those
who found it; 'Itravel', to purchase bus tickets electronically;

'DroneAfrica', the first drone service in Cameroon primarily used to map the agricultural sector; and 'SmartFinance', an app enabling money transactions between credit unions and their clients. Such applications are often in their infant stages but young entrepreneurs are inspired by the success stories of their elders.

In Cameroon, most streets are unnamed and few locations have an address. Taxi-drivers respond to directions such as 'drop me off near the pink building downtown' or the name of popular bars, hotels, and markets. In 2016, Aymard Bamal, a member of ActivSpaces in Douala, created the application 'Cloomify' after losing a relative who died from hypertension before the emergency medical services could locate his home.[78]

Photo 14. Example of a digital address in Ghana: 'A' refers to the region (Ashanti), 'K' refers to the district (Kumasi), 5028 is the unique address within the postal code (AK-039)

The app allows users to locate a site based on a given distance but unlike Google maps it does not necessitate internet access. Bamal invested 2 million CFA ($4,625) and had teams on bicycles roaming around Douala with cameras filming at a 360-degree angle to register each site. In 2016, Cloomify earned second place for best mobile innovation at the 'AppsAfrica Innovation Awards' held in South Africa and after a year the app already had over 5,000 users. Its creators have been contacted to develop the same initiative in other West African countries. In Ghana the national government sponsored the information technology firm, Vocakom, to develop a similar application. In 2017, the Ghana Post GPS mobile application was launched to provide for the first time an address and postal codes for every location in the country (see photo 14).[79] At the same time in Nairobi, Kenya an Uber-style online platform – called 'Flare' – was created to track private ambulance crews and fire trucks to connect people to the closest emergency responders. Despite a $15 yearly membership cost for individuals – a hefty sum by local standards – 'Flare' is particularly useful in a country where there are more than 50 different numbers for emergency services and the app significantly decreases emergency response times.[80] Rising entrepreneurs at ActivSpaces are aware of these inventions and draw inspiration from local initiatives which are increasingly having an impact at the regional level.

Two applications that seemed particularly innovative and useful at the 2016 ActivSpaces gathering were 'Feem' and 'Heritage'. 'Feem' is an application to share files using wifi. It differs from airdrop in that it is not limited to IPhones and Macs – rare commodities in Cameroon – but is available on all mobile phones that can access a wifi hotspot. 'Feem' is regarded as a 'success story' in the Cameroonian world of app development.[81] Its founder, Fritz Ekwoge, is from Buea, and he first began 'coding' at 14-years-old during school hours as he created programmes on his Ti-82 calculator. Now with over 1 million downloads, his application is one of the highest-selling in Cameroon and even in the wider West African region. Most 'Feem' users, however, are not Cameroonians, as almost all of them are in India, Europe and the United States. This transnational success came as a big surprise to its founder, who built the application with Cameroonian realities in mind, based on the knowledge that wifi or wifi-hotspots in Cameroon usually provide much more rapid browsing than a regular internet connection. Yet, in Cameroon 'Feem' is scarcely used, and those who use it most are students to rapidly transfer files so they can cheat on tests. While attempting to meet the needs of Cameroonians, Ekwoge explained that he was also trying to show that Cameroonians can create and export, rather than being confined solely to the role of consumers. In that, he succeeded, but not in responding to the needs of his fellow citizens.

The co-founder of ActivSpaces, Valéry Colong, also aims to tailor app development to the local realities of Cameroonians. To do so, he is working on creating an app called 'Heritage'. Colong thought of 'Heritage' when he became a father and wondered how he would transmit cultural values to his child. Colong himself cannot speak his mother's native tongue and his spouse cannot speak any African languages, so 'it became clear to me [him] that we as young Africans are failing on the side of culture and tradition'.[82] An increasing number of young Cameroonians like Colong are raised in modernizing urban areas rather than in rural dwellings surrounded by their kin. As such, his application is meant to familiarize the youth with certain aspects of their cultural traditions through tutorial videos and lessons in various forms. 'Heritage' is a modern way to uphold tradition and could also be very useful to Cameroonians in the diaspora facing such concerns. Yet, once again it remains to be seen whether this innovative concept made with local realities in mind addresses the needs and wants of Cameroonians.

The case of Kingsley illustrates some of the realities faced by the average Cameroonian. Kingsley is a young man in his twenties who lives with his uncle and his children in a small shack, located not far from the offices of ActivSpaces in Buea. His mother having recently passed away, he needed to support himself financially, so he left his village near Bamenda to find work in Buea. In Buea, Kingsley applied for a job and was asked for his phone number, but he no longer owned a phone as children in his village broke his previous one. He was told that without a phone number it would be impossible to reach him after his application had been reviewed. Despite the low-cost of mobile phones, Kingsley had spent most of his savings traveling to Buea and could not afford to allocate 5,000 CFA to purchase a mobile phone when he depended on the generosity of others for food. Thus, Kingsley turned to the informal sector – no application or phone number required – and found a job as a construction builder with a weekly salary of 10,000 CFA ($18.10). With this money he hopes to buy 'any phone, just an 'allo-allo'', so he can apply for another job. Despite living a few minutes away from the offices of ActivSpaces, Kingsley has never heard of the tech-hub and, when brought up, Kingsley showed little interest – even a slight distrust – towards these costly mobile innovations. He claimed that a standard phone was enough to 'help me change my life. We know that ants can bite you and you die, so we shouldn't minimize them just like we shouldn't minimize cellphones'.[83] Even if Kingsley could afford a smartphone to access mobile applications, his life of subsistence – like that of most Cameroonians – creates a sense of disconnect from the applications created by young technology savy entrepreneurs in Buea, as if they are 'not for him' even when, in fact, they are.

Kingsley is not alone. During my visit in Nyakokombo, the local midwife was not aware of the app 'GiftedMom', even though the mobile-health platform is directly related to her work and has earned many awards and international attention with reports from the BBC and RFI. 'GiftedMom' is an SMS service with 2,100 subscribers destined to help expectant and new mothers in rural-communities receive advice about their health and perinatal appointments.[84] Its co-founder, Alain Nteff, has been hailed by CNN as the '23 year old savior of Cameroon's mothers' on his way to 'wiping out maternal mortality'.[85] The midwife in Nyakokombo acknowledges that the mobile application would be of great use as she currently keeps handwritten files with the prenatal appointments of expectant mothers. When her patients do not show, she has to give them a call as a reminder. Likewise, the app 'Ndolo360', which allows users to ask questions about sexual and reproductive health anonymously, could have a significant impact in a country where 40% of pregnancies are estimated to be unintended and 14% of deaths among women of reproductive age are due to maternal causes.[86] In sub-Saharan Africa, the risk of dying during pregnancy or childbirth is one in 38, which is about 100 times more than in the developed world where the likelihood of dying is one in 3,700.[87] Each year tens of thousands of Cameroonian women in rural areas also die of breast and cervical cancers due to a lack of screening, diagnosis and sufficient medical treatment. In 2017, the co-founder of 'GiftedMom', Conrad Tankou launched 'CerviScan' which uses a low-cost digital microscope – operating on battery so it can be used in the most remote enclaves – to obtain on-site analysis of tissue samples and identify cancerous tumors.[88] The 'CerviScan' is equipped with a digital camera that transmits live images to a smartphone or tablet which are then downloaded by Cameroonian oncologists at partner hospitals. In a few months, this innovation allowed 1,200 women to receive free screening and to diagnose early stages of cancer for 100 women in villages where sanitary facilities are non-existent. Tankou plans to cover 50 villages by the end of 2018. In the meantime, the midwife and the majority of villagers in Nyakokombo have not heard of 'CerviScan' and those who have – including urban dwellers – often react like Kingsley and reject these mobile applications, preferring to stick with their habits and not run the risk of incurring more costs. The vast majority of villagers cannot afford or do not see the necessity of owning a smartphone to download other mobile applications like 'GiftedMom' or 'Ndolo360'. Even when applications would directly meet certain needs, consumers are often unaware that they exist and they are primarily accessible to Cameroonians who own smartphones.

The founder of 'Feem' attributes a lack of awareness from the population to the difficulties of marketing in Cameroon.[89]

Yet, applications like 'Feem' or 'GiftedMom' usually necessitate an Android-type phone, and only 19% of villagers surveyed in Nyakokombo owned one. This is representative of the overall Cameroonian population, as in 2014 only 18% of Cameroonians owned a smart-phone (Tchakounté 2014). Mobile applications cannot be accessed by the vast majority of Cameroonians and, in turn, do not have a large-scale impact on societal development (Chéneau-Loquay 2010: 34). Even when they do pinpoint the needs of their fellow citizens, entrepreneurs are only targeting about a fifth of the overall Cameroonian population. In two years, from 2014 to 2016, the number of smartphone connections in sub-Saharan Africa has doubled to nearly 200 million, yet it still only accounts for a quarter of mobile connections in the region.[90] This segment of the population is primarily composed of urban dwellers, thus mobile apps also tend to enhance rural-urban social inequalities. Downloading applications on smartphones has also led to an augmentation in mobile malware prevalence, as users often download malicious software disguised as legitimate applications – further enhancing feelings of distrust towards these innovations (Tchakounté 2014: 3). ActivSpaces receives minimal positive publicity or financial support from the central government and is dependent on funding from NGOs and other charitable donors. While in certain countries like Kenya, Nigeria and South-Africa a start-up culture and successful innovations have formed, in Cameroon start-ups are struggling to scale up and ActivSpaces risks collapsing as a result of sustained government ordered internet shutdowns in Buea – stalling all tech-related activities. Certain mobile applications encounter glitches, to the dismay of users who paid for them, and when the mobile application is free users tend to doubt its reliability. A common refrain amongst the population is that one should not trust something if it is not advised by his kin. Due to a combination of the aforementioned factors, a culture of trust towards mobile applications is slow to emerge in Cameroon. However, as smartphones continue to become more affordable, penetration improves in rural areas and app-developers pinpoint the needs of local communities, the distrust surrounding mobile applications in Cameroon is likely to gradually dissipate and such innovations will become ingrained in the routines of Cameroonians. Nonetheless, for the time being it appears that many have overloaded expectations for mobile applications to drive economic growth – in line with 'technological determinism' train of thought – and a perceived mobile fracture has formed between modern mobile applications and Cameroonian societal norms and habits.

## Notes

Countrymeters.info. 'Cameroon Population'. *Countrymeters*, accessed July 20, 2018.

14    'Human Development Reports'. | *Human Development Reports.*

15    Max Smith, 'Mobile Telephony and Local Agency: Cameroonian Ways of Appropriation', (SIT Cameroon Independent Study Project, 2016.)

16    Members of the informal sector surveyed in this study are a combination of merchants and unemployed individuals. The vast majority of the unemployed partake in informal activities, which represent a sector of the economy that is 'not taxed, monitored by any form of government, or included in any gross national product (GNP).' As such, the line between merchants who do not

17    CIA World Factbook, 2016.

18    Countrymeters.info. 'Cameroon Population.' *Countrymeters.*

19    'Cameroon: Orange and MTN Monopolize 93.8% of the Telephone Market'. *Business in Cameroon*, 7 Feb. 2016.

20    'Welcome to Orange Cameroon'. *About Orange Cameroon | Orange Cameroun*, and *Business in Cameroon*, 'Cameroon: Orange and MTN'.

21    *Business in Cameroon*, 'Cameroon: Orange and MTN', 7 Feb. 2016.

22    Ibid.

23 'Suspended since Two Weeks, Vodafone Cameroon Submit a Request for License'. *Business in Cameroon*. 26 Sept. 2017.

24 'Cameroon's Mobile Penetration Hits 80%'. *Telecompaper*, 12 Feb. 2016.

25 Interview with Ngae Denis in Yaoundé, The Director of Infrastructures and Networks access at the MINPOSTE, 11/10/16

26 'Cameroon: Orange and MTN Monopolise 93.8% of the Telephone Market'. *Business in Cameroon*, 7 Feb. 2016; Interview with CamTel Bamenda Service Head for Technical Matters, 17/10/16

27 'The General Conference of the International Labour Organization'. *International Labour Organization*, 2002.

28 'Cameroon: Poverty Reduction Strategy Paper'. *The International Monetary Fund*, 2010.

29 Interview with Proxy on Avenue Kennedy, phone salesman, 11/25/16

30 Ibid.

31 'Annuaire Statistique du Cameroun, édition 2015', Institut National de la Statistique, 354

32 Interview with call-boxer in Fang, 11/13/16

33 Most call-boxers have one phone to transfer credit for each mobile phone operator, as such one of the call-boxers I interviewed had 5 phones (the fifth phone was used for calls only)

34 Interview with Professor Walter Gam Nkwi in Buea, 11/18/16

35 Interview with call-boxer in Yaoundé, 11/09/16

36 Cheap whisky sachets banned since 2014 for their deleterious health effects. For more on banned whisky sachets see: Roland Muma. 'Cameroon Bans Consumption of Whisky Sachets for Health Reasons'. *Face2Face Africa*, 10 May 2014.

37 Interview with Nkwi, 11/18/16 (note: 'mobile' also in the sense that many are now ambulant)

38 'Cameroon to Increase Minimum Wage from De 28,000 to 36,270 FCFA'. *Business in Cameroon*, 22 July 2014.

39 Amongst all participants, 67% owned one mobile phone, 28% owned two and 5% owned three. The price of these phones varied as 53% of them cost between 0-20,000 CFA, 22% between 20,001-40,000 CFA,

13% between 40,001-60,000 CFA, 3% between 80,001-100,000 CFA and 8% above 100,000 CFA (1% did not answer.)

40   'The Android generation', term used by Paul Biya to describe the Cameroonian Youth during a speech on February 10th, 2016. In this study, 33% of participants owned Android phones, 50% owned standard phones  and 17% owned both.

41   'Memory Cards 20 Products Found'. *Memory Cards - Buy Online | Jumia Cameroun.*

42   Sophie Eastaugh. 'Solar-Cart Can Charge 80 Cell Phones at Once'. *CNN*, Cable News Network, 24 Oct. 2017.

43   Interview with Teacher in Nyakokombo, 11/12/16

44   An inhabitant of Nyakokombo earning the national minimum wage, who decides to buy a 10,000 CFA standard phone; a 2,500 CFA memory card; a 16,500 CFA solar panel package and 500 CFA worth of credit a week, will spend up to 53,000 CFA towards his new device despite earning 435,240 CFA a year (12.2%.)

45   Interview with Teacher in Nyakokombo, 11/12/16 'It [phone] creates disorder because the students when you give lectures they play, they follow their music and others can enter a non-decent website, pornography'

46   'L'interdiction des téléphones portables à l'école fait aussi débat à l'étranger'. *Le Monde.fr*, Le Monde, 14 Dec. 2017.

47   'My dear listen, the telephone has become a real danger for couples. Telephone has ruined marriages, telephone has ruined households, telephone has spread fights. Sorry don't touch your boy's phone'

48   Jake Nicol, et al. 'Inside the Vast (and Growing) Global Trade in Stolen Smart Phones'. *National Geographic*, National Geographic Society, 9 Sept. 2015.

49   Gerry Smith. 'Left to Die ... All for The Sake of a Mobile Phone'. *The Huffington Post*, TheHuffingtonPost.com, 25 Jan. 2014.

50   Interview with Professor Walter Gam Nkwi at the University of Buea, 11/18/16

51   M&G Africa. 'There Are Always Surprises: 11 Bank-Breaking Facts about Mobile Money and Africa'. *MG Africa*, 29 Feb. 2016.

52   Ibid; 'Global Findex Data: Sub-Saharan Africa'. *The World Bank*, 2014.

53   Questionnaire Chief of Orange Agency in Bamenda, 11/10/16

54   *Business in Cameroon*: 'Mobile Money Ready for Takeoff in Cameroon', 3.

55   Ibid, 6; sub-Saharan Africa has the lowest level of financial inclusion with only about 21% of the adult population having a bank account compared to 34% in Latin American and the Caribbean and 90% in the OECD. Jacob Oduor et al. 'Capital Requirement, Bank Competition and Stability in Africa.' *Review of Development Finance*, vol. 7, no. 1, (June 2017), pp. 45–51.

56   Ibid.

57   'Afrique: ces applications agricoles qui boostent le Ghana'. *Le Point Afrique*, 9 Jan. 2018.

58   Ndubuisi Ekekwe. 'How Digital Technology Is Changing Farming in Africa'. *Harvard Business Review*, 18 May 2017.

59   Christine Dell'amore. 'The Humans of the Bird World'. *National Geographic*, National Geographic Society, June 2018.

60   SIT class with traditional doctors, 10/24/16: 'you must believe to heal, if you don't believe you will not heal'

61   Phoebe Parke. 'How Many People Use Social Media in Africa?' *CNN*, Cable News Network, 14 Jan. 2016.

62   'Africa Internet Users, 2017 Population and Facebook Statistics.' *Internet World Stats*.

63   Tied with Facebook-messenger for most monthly active users (in millions). 'Most Popular Messaging Apps 2017'. *Statista.*

64   92% of participants in this study who listed why they used applications said it was to communicate and 42% also said it was to learn and follow the news.

65   'Cameroon is Cameroon', Interview with Mathieu Youbi in Yaoundé, Founder of LCCLC, 24/11/16

66   Ibid.

67   Daily Mail : 'Pregnant woman left to die on steps of Cameroon hospital because she had no money to pay for treatment as relatives tried to in vain to deliver twins alive', 03/14/16.

68   For more on the use of mobile phones during the Arab Spring see: Heather Brown et al. 'The Role of Social Media in the Arab Uprisings'. *Pew Research Center's Journalism Project*, 28 Nov. 2012.

69   Kieron Monks. 'Cameroon Goes Offline after Anglophone Revolt'. *CNN*, Cable News Network, 2 Jan. 2018.

70   Interview with Professor Moussa Njoya at the University of Yaoundé, 30/11/16

71   'Cameroun: Le gouvernement va en guerre contre la propagation des fausses nouvelles sur internet.' *TIC Mag*, 16 Jan. 2017.

72   Interview with Dr. Michael Soney in Buea, Director of the College of Technology at Buea University, 11/17/16

73   Interview with Professor Akama at the University of Buea, 11/16/16

74   Interview with Christian, Assistant Lecturer at the College of Technology at the University of Buea, 11/17/16; Interview with Dr. Blaise Nande at the University of Buea, 11/15/16

75   Interview with Dr. Michael Soney in Buea, Director of the College of Technology at Buea University, 11/17/16

76   'Welcome to 'Silicon Mountain', Africa's next Tech Hub'. *The France 24 Observers*, France 24, 23 Sept. 2016; 'Buea, la Silicon Valley du Cameroun - BBC Afrique'. *BBC News*, BBC.

77   Interview with Chawa in Buea, Student at the University of Buea, 11/16/16

78   Cyril Bensimon. 'Au Cameroun, pour continuer de rayonner, Douala contrainte de se réinventer'. *Le Monde.fr*, Le Monde, 23 Aug. 2017.

79   Delali Adogla-Bessa. 'Nana Addo Launches Ghana's Digital Property Address System'. *Citifmonline.com*, 18 Oct. 2017.

80   Catharina Moh. 'How a Speedy Emergency Services App Is Saving Lives'. *BBC News*, BBC, 24 Nov. 2017.

81   Interview with Fritz Ekwoge at the Annual gathering of ActivSpaces in Buea, Founder of *Feem*, 11/16/16

82   Interview with Valéry Colong at the Annual Gathering of ActivSpaces in Buea, Co-Founder of ActivSpaces, 11/16/16

83   Interview with Kingsley in Buea, 11/17/16

84   SMS is the abbreviation for Short Message Service

85 Milena Veselinovic. 'This 23-Year-Old Is Saving Mothers with an App'. *CNN*, Cable News Network, 17 Feb. 2015.

86 'Mobile App Breaks Sex Taboos in Cameroon - Page 2 of 3'. *Working Woman Report*, 2 Oct. 2016; Veselinovic. 'Saving Mothers with an App', 17 Feb. 2015.

87 Veselinovic. 'Saving Mothers with an App', 17 Feb. 2015.

88 Samir Abdelkrim. 'Au Cameroun, comment une start-up lutte contre les cancers féminins'. *Le Monde.fr*, Le Monde, 7 June 2018.

89 Interview with Fritz Ekwoge at the Annual Gathering of ActivSpaces in Buea, Founder of *Feem*, 11/16/16

90 GSMA. *The Mobile Economy – sub-Saharan Africa, 2017*, 3.

# Chapter 3

## Corporate Acculturation: Case Study of MTN-Guinea

### A. Introduction

The responses of groups to acculturation vary and are identified in Robert Redfield's *Memorandum* as falling either under 'acceptance, adaptation or reaction'. *Acceptance* refers to the taking over of another culture and the surrender of groups which accept the loss of cultural heritage in the process of assimilating foreign values or goods. *Adaptation* is when both original and foreign traits are combined to produce a functioning cultural whole and the reworking of patterns from the two cultures. *Reaction* denotes the rise of anti-acculturative movements as a result of oppression or the unforeseen consequences of the acceptance of foreign traits (Redfield et al. 1936: 152). The acculturation of mobile-phones in Guinea and wider West Africa broadly falls in the category of *adaptation*. As Charles Ess notes in *Culture, Technology, Communication* (Ess 2001: 25), the increase in cultural transactions is correlated with the intercultural synthesis of the global and the local – i.e. 'glocalization' (as discussed in Chapter 1). More than ever, the rise of ICTs has led corporations, including mobile telecommunications companies such as MTN, to take into consideration the local context of the countries where they operate and bridge local and global culture(s) to sell their products. The concept of 'corporate acculturation', addressed through the case study of MTN in Guinea-Conakry, refers to the process by which mobile telephony companies adapt their operations, such as marketing and sales, to the cultural traits or social patterns of the country in which they operate and, in turn, reshape them.

77

## B. Setting for the Field Research

To understand the process of corporate acculturation of mobile telephony, a month of research was conducted within Africa's biggest telecoms company, MTN.[91] MTN is a South African multinational mobile operator which in 2016 ranked as

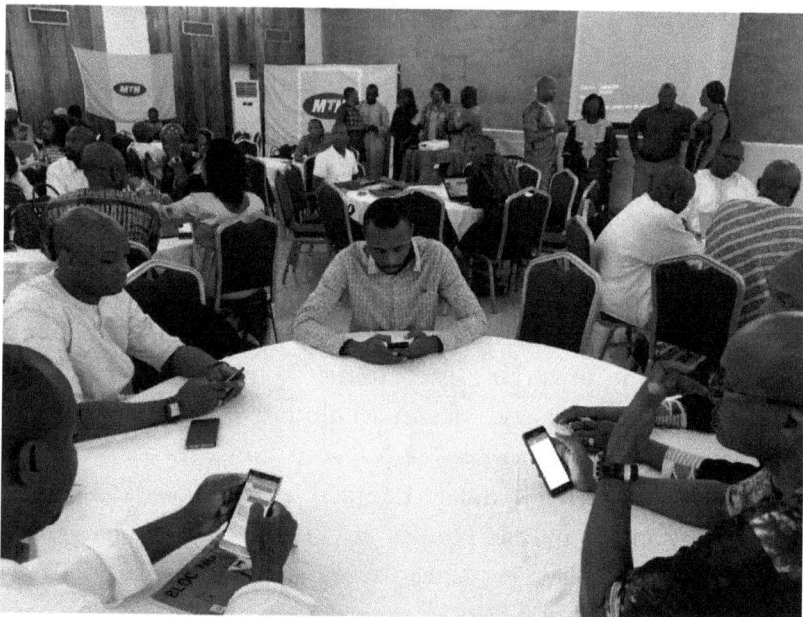

Photo 15. MTN employees on their smartphones prior to a meeting

the most 'admired and valuable' African brand and has 240 million subscribers across Africa and the Middle East.[92] The company employs a total of 20,000 personnel, representing over 60 different nationalities (see photo 15).[93] Formerly known in Guinea as Areeba, which is still how most customers refer to the company, MTN entered the Guinean telephony market in 2006. The company is widely regarded as having brought mobile telephony to the country, as it reduced the price of the SIM card from 1 million Guinean francs ($110) to 3,000 GNF ($0.33).[94] Since 2013, however, MTN has lost its leadership of the telecommunications market to Orange. In 2017, with over 6 million subscribers, Orange controlled 58% of market shares, MTN 23%, Cellcom 19% and Intercel 1%.[95] Guinea is a frontier market, in the sense that the spread of mobile telephony is relatively recent, business regulations are still at low levels of maturity, and the country is economically one of the least developed in the world.[96] This makes Guinea a prime case study to analyze the acculturation of mobile telephony, as the telephony market is still relatively dormant compared to that of Cameroon and has the potential for rapid growth and outsized returns for mobile operators. Additionally, in 2017 the South-African CEO of MTN-Guinea was replaced by a Senegalese who arrived with the mandate to better suit MTN's offers to West African dynamics. Towards that end, new heads of departments from Ghana, Cameroon and Guinea were named and are bringing diversity in approaches to problems which are similar throughout West Africa.

The CEO of MTN-Guinea, Papa Sow, believes that the nomination of more West African employees will improve channels of vertical communication and feedback between agents on the ground and the hierarchy.[97] Sow explains that in West Africa, unlike his experiences in Central Africa, the 'boss' is expected to be accessible, humble and accompany his agents in their endeavors, which is why upon his arrival he organized weekly breakfasts with members from each department. Heads of departments are also acculturating to the local environment and getting acquainted with their agents. Following his arrival, Lawrence Ngalah, the head of Sales and Distribution, engaged in a month-long country-wide road trip to regional headquarters. Newcomers must also be aware of local corporate practices such as 'casual Fridays', when most employees tend to wear African fabrics. Or the fact that the work week ends at noon on Fridays as not to miss the 'Jumu'ah', the most important prayer of the week for Muslims. Not only is mobile telephony acculturated to its local environment but so are the employees and internal structure of the mobile company itself. MTN-Guinea engages in structural corporate adaptations and exercises 'strategic agency' in acculturating mobile telephony to local realities. In doing so, the company shapes and sets the field for the consumer appropriation – 'tactical agency' – of mobile telephony. To illustrate this process, this chapter draws on field research conducted inland, in the cities of Kindia (Western region) and Mamou (Central region), as well as 37 formal interviews with MTN employees across the ten different departments that make up the companies' headquarters in "Kaloum" – the administrative center of the capital Conakry. This research primarily examines the corporate structures put in place by mobile operators through the process of 'interconnection', as well as marketing and sales strategies employed by MTN in this 'game of mirrors' of adapting to the local demand and cultural codes of consumers while reshaping them.

## C. Local 'Interconnection'

In Guinea, like in Cameroon, mobile operators and the state-controlled Regulating Authority of Posts and Telecommunications (RAPT) charge subscribers additional costs for 'off-network' communications from one cell phone company to another. Despite the rise of private mobile operators since 2006, the government's importance in the mobile telephony market lies in its monopoly over the 'National Optical Fiber Backbone', as it is in charge of laying out the infrastructure that will provide 'interconnection' between mobile telephony operators.[98] As made clear by the head of Information Technology (IT) of MTN-Guinea, Reuben Opata, laying out telecommunication infrastructure is the first stage in the implementation of mobile telephony and follows global communications standards set by the International Telecommunication Union (ITU). However, Opata explains that while IT largely operates as an 'enabler', the second stage of implementation is the corporate adaptation of mobile telephony to the local environment and specificities, i.e. acculturation. In that vein, the fact that communications between subscribers of different companies cost more than those within the same company, and each operator sets its own rates, is purely a business decision geared towards controlling market power.

Like in Cameroon and most of West Africa, subscribers in Guinea incur the costs of interconnection. Since 2016, Orange has charged an additional 200 GNF ($0.022) per minute on calls to MTN while MTN charges an additional 167 GNF ($0.2) for calls to Orange. Due to these business-marketing decisions, which often change, Guineans own multiple SIMs from the different operators, and 86% of calls are made 'on-network', as they have learned to check which company their contacts subscribe to.[99] In Guinea, the first digits of all MTN phone numbers start with '66' and Orange numbers start with '62'. While late payment is common, at the end of each month MTN and Orange are supposed to pay each other the difference between outgoing and incoming calls. Currently, Orange holds most of the market, so their clients call amongst themselves and the company has to pay a smaller 'off-network' fee to other operators. In Guinea and other West African nations, such a system of interconnection increases the risks of a mobile company exercising a near monopoly on the local telecommunications market.

The new CEO of MTN-Guinea acknowledges that Orange was able to overtake leadership of the telephony market by being more in touch with West African specificities and investing in rural areas. Close to 40% of the Guinea population resides in urban areas, and Conakry alone accounts for 60% of national revenue for the telephony market. Yet, Orange recognized that the market in Conakry was saturated and that the 'urban guerilla war' with MTN would be won by investing in villages, as urbanites would subscribe to the same company as their rural kin.[100] Furthermore, MTN chose to invest in Worldwide Interoperability for Microwave Access (Wi-MAX) technology rather than 3G for its internet services. Wi-MAX is similar to Wi-Fi in that it allows users to connect to the internet without wires. Unlike Wi-Fi, Wi-MAX can cover larger geographic locations and was introduced in 2001 as an alternative to cable and Digital Subscriber Line (DSL).[101] Yet, Wi-MAX is not compatible with local realities in Guinea as the technology is dependent on stable power sources. Accordingly, Wi-MAX have primarily been adopted by companies and wealthy subscribers, many of which own electric generators. Instead of significantly increasing internet penetration in Guinea, Wi-MAX have now become an 'end of life' product.

In 2017, MTN ceased restocking Wi-MAX to introduce 'Wifi-pockets', which are small mobile hotspots better suited to local needs. The use of 'wifi-pockets' for access to internet on mobile phones will continue to fuel the rise of online communication services such as Facebook or WhatsApp – which both provide free call and messaging services. 'Wifi-pockets' have the potential to affect the system of 'interconnection', as easier access to Facebook and WhatsApp will gradually decrease the need for subscribers to hold multiple SIMs in order to take advantage of price differentials. As network coverage continues to improve, easier internet access has led subscribers to increasingly use WhatsApp or Facebook to send messages and reduces the need for multiple SIMs to ensure connectivity. In all, 'interconnection' is an example of how governmental and corporate structures, as well as marketing decisions like the implementation of 'wifi-pockets', continuously shape consumer appropriation of mobile telephony in Guinea.

## D. The Call-Box System and Credit Distribution Chain

The credit distribution and SIM registration system set in place by mobile operators are other significant examples of corporate acculturation to local realities, which end up reshaping consumer appropriation. In Guinea, 99.5% of mobile subscriptions are pre-paid, meaning that consumers purchase credit or internet data on a daily basis rather than subscribing to a monthly plan.[102] This phenomenon, common throughout sub-Saharan Africa, is largely due to the lack of a monthly steady income for the majority of the population and because it enables access for populations without credit records, fixed addresses, or reliable income. However, even High Value Customers (HVC) with a significant income prefer pre-paid to post-paid subscriptions that bind them to long-term contracts in a volatile market constantly altered by new marketing decisions. The CEO of MTN identifies the high rates of pre-paid subscriptions as being revelatory of local mindsets, i.e. the distrust of consumers towards private companies like mobile operators and the habit 'of making purchases based on daily needs, not knowing what tomorrow will hold'.[103] With these local particularities in mind, mobile operators have structured a credit distribution chain that permits the dissemination of credit on most street corners, at Points of Sales (POS) and 'call-boxes'.[104] Mobile operators have subcontracted the distribution of credit to companies which sit at the top of the chain and are called 'distributors'. Major distributors in Conakry can supply around 400,000,000 GNF ($44,000) of credit per day to the 'dealers', 'sub-dealers', and POS or 'call-boxers' below them.

The call-box system in Guinea, as in Cameroon, was established by mobile operators in the early days of mobile telephony. Today, subscribers no longer use the call-box to call at lower rates but rather to buy credit or to make mobile money transactions. As a result of the rapidity of such transfers, credit has come to be known as 'taf-taf'. Such renaming, or local branding, is common in West Africa. Whereas phones used only for basic services – calling and receiving – are referred to as 'allo-allo' in Cameroon, they are known as 'Bambeto-Cosa' in Guinea. The name was inspired by the standard Motorola mobile phones that first flooded the Guinean telecommunication market. These phones were so cheap and had such extended battery life that even the residents of Bambeto and Cosa – two neighborhoods in Conakry notorious for their strikes and lower standards of living – could afford to buy one, charge it in-between power outages, and purchase 'taf-taf'.[105] In Conakry and other cities, most call-boxers and POS call their suppliers in the morning and ask for a certain amount of 'taf-taf' to be sent electronically. However, this varies based on levels of trust, and late payments often lead suppliers to request the money before transferring the credit. The fact that most POS own boutiques with a wide range of products, also often impedes the smooth supply of credit distribution.

Photo 16. Ngalah (right) at a POS in Kindia

In Kindia, a major POS at a busy intersection had over 1 million GNF ($110) to spend on credit. However, his 'sub-dealer' had not come by in weeks and the POS did not want to incur the financial costs and bothersome task of leaving his store.[106] Lawrence Ngalah called the sub-dealer, who arrived in less than five minutes prompting Ngalah to ask why he did not come more often if he could do so as rapidly (see photo 16). The lesson is largely lost on the sub-dealer who does not speak French. Nonetheless, Ngalah returns to the POS and explains that cellular credit is like water, oil, flour and the other products he sells – so he should not wait for his stock to be exhausted before replenishing it. The POS concurs but reminds Ngalah that unlike a shortage of flour he is still distilling Orange credit and generating enough income that he does not feel the need to track down his sub-dealer for MTN credit. By using the same sub-dealers and POS, mobile operators face such risks. Overall, pre-paid practices and the informality of the credit distribution chain is a double edge sword as their adaptability is also often at the root of a lack of efficiency. Across the street another POS had gone to Conakry leaving his little brother in charge of the store and the credit dormant, as his sibling did not know how to make the transfers. As a result of the missing sub-dealer and traveling POS, the entire intersection was short of MTN credit.

## E. SIM Registration and 'SIM-Box' Frauds

Similar to the credit distribution chain, mobile operators tailored the SIM registration process to local realities. Knowing that many Guineans do not carry or even own an identity card, especially in rural areas or amongst the youth below 18 years old (the legal age for an ID card), operators did not require registration to buy a SIM prior to 2016. In Africa, SIM registration laws were first introduced in 2006. Prior to then subscribers across the continent were able to purchase a prepaid card and use it more or less anonymously.[107] Yet, it was not until the last couple of years that most regulations have gone into effect. MTN-Guinea sought to facilitate the process by forming 'Foot Soldier' (FS) units, led by supervisors, who walk around certain assigned sectors to register new subscribers (see photo

17). In doing so, FS limit the transportation costs for potential subscribers and appeal to locally-valued forms of human interaction by physically reaching out to their customers.[108] FS units are taught that 'if a man is not wearing a shirt, then he must be trying to buy a SIM'.[109] This saying reflects on the democratization of mobile telephony and that even the poorest are willing to make sacrifices to subscribe to a mobile operator. With that in mind, FS should appeal to all customers no matter the appearance. However, this system of registration and local agency gave way to new forms of criminal activities such as 'SIM Box' frauds.

Photo 17. FS unit in Kindia during lunch break

'SIM Box' frauds are the use by fraudsters of hundreds of pre-paid SIM cards to terminate international calls through local phone numbers and thus bypass all international interconnect charges.[110] Operators lose significant revenue and subscribers associate the poor quality of the call with the brand. Furthermore, 'SIM Box' frauds have reinforced anxieties linked to the anonymity of mobile phones and rumors of sorcery leading to 'killer mobile phone numbers' (Bonhomme 2012). The rumor of killer numbers is believed to have been birthed in Nigeria, three years after the introduction of GSM technology in the country. In July 2004, in the city of Calabar, a young boy answered a call from an unidentified phone number and heard a man coughing on the other end of the line before losing consciousness. His sister rushed to pick up the phone only to collapse as well. A journalist inquired about the incident and called back the alleged murderous number, only to speak to a woman who threatened to cover him with the blood of Jesus but he did not collapse. Nonetheless, as a product of the 'radio trottoir' culture in West Africa, the rumor soon spread to surrounding nations that calls from some unidentified phone numbers could instantly kill those receiving the call. Variants of the so-called 'killer numbers' have also spread panics in other parts of the world. Most notably in 2007, in Pakistan, it was believed that such numbers could trigger impotence in men and pregnancy in women. Similar messages spread throughout Asia, the Middle East and Africa. The rumors reached such proportions that MTN-Ghana, the largest cellular network in the country, released a statement assuring subscribers that 'a full scale national and international priority investigation has been conducted in the last 48 hours' and that 'the investigation has confirmed that these rumors are completely unsubstantiated and have no technological evidence to support them'.[111] In other West African countries, mobile operators have issued similar statements yet text messages such as the following from Nigeria continue to circulate: 'Please, don't pick up any call with 09141 its instant death after the call, 7 people have died already. Please tell others fast, it's urgent'.[112] Such hoaxes continue to crop up and to this day the fear of 'killer numbers' persists in Guinea and the wider West African region.

Since the advent of mobile telephony in Africa, the lack of subscriber registration has allowed fraudsters to purchase unlimited amounts of SIMs and make calls from unidentified phone numbers. Along with 'killer numbers' and 'SIM Box' subscriber registration has also raised concerns with regards to terrorism in the wider region of West Africa. In 2015, Nigerian authorities followed the lead of other developing economic centers, such as Kenya and India, and demanded that all mobile operators collect biometric information from SIM buyers and disconnect all unregistered SIMs.[113] In India, Kenya and Nigeria, the interest of national security and the threat of terrorism was at the source of these regulations. The absence of SIM registration permitted terrorists to act under the cover of anonymity during the November 2008 attacks in Mubai, the September 2013 attack on a gate mall in Nairobi and during attacks by Boko Haram insurgents. In Nigeria, MTN disconnected 3.1 million of the 5.1 million unregistered SIMs and was fined $1.7 billion for not reaching the government's demands.[114] Suffering from the fallout of this fine and the volatility of Nigerian currency and global oil prices, MTN's progress in Nigeria, which accounts for a quarter of MTN's 240 million subscribers, has stalled and the largest mobile operator in Africa almost sunk.

The case of MTN-Nigeria served as a strong warning to mobile operators throughout West Africa, as many national governments and regulatory bodies have now implemented similar policies.[115] In 2016, the Guinean RAPT demanded that operators end the sale of pre-activated SIMs and delete within a week all numbers that were not registered with an ID and birth certificate. By the end of 2016, MTN's newly formed registration team worked with the Information Technology department to disable over 400,000 SIMs with faulty registration.[116] Despite the costs of registering users, mobile operators stand to benefit from such government-mandated policies. The introduction of SIM registration rules is burdensome and increases switching costs, thereby reducing the common practice of swapping SIMs and 'churn' rates, which is the term used to describe dormant subscribers who have migrated to competing operators.[117] SIM registration has also reduced the popular practice of purchasing a local SIM when travelling internationally, known as 'plastic roaming', which prevents mobile operators from profiting off international calls. 'Plastic roaming' may eventually altogether disappear as since the 'Transform Africa' Kigali summit in 2013, telecommunication regulators have worked on creating a unique mobile telephony network throughout Africa. This network would allow subscribers to travel from one country to another without having to switch to a local SIM and would cancel the coast of roaming for inter-African mobile communications. While the project is still in its early stages, in 2016 it was tested in Rwanda, South Sudan, Uganda, and Kenya, for a significant increase in traffic and revenue for operators.[118] Furthermore, mobile operators can now use registration to gain insight on their subscribers and tailor their services and products to individual customers. For example, MTN often sends a message and bonuses to their subscribers on their birthday. The Customer Relations department also calls High Value customers to thank them for their fidelity, ask about their hobbies and advertise new promotions. The SIM registration process has been reshaped by local realities and, in turn, is changing subscriber habits.

Faulty subscriber registration is often due to the poor quality of photos with biometric information sent by FS and POS to the registration team at the MTN headquarters and the fact that agents must activate the SIM within two hours following the purchase. This measure is designed to allow subscribers to use their newly-acquired SIM at once. However, in rural areas with limited mobile phone service, MTN-agents are often unable to activate the SIM within the required time frame. To the great dismay of subscribers who have bought a SIM and provided the required biometric information – their SIM can be disconnected a few days after purchase or never even be activated at all. In 2017, MTN responded to this issue by adopting a new version of a mobile platform, called 'Axon', which not only shines a green dial to verify the quality of the photos taken but also allows FS and POS to register subscribers off-line and activate their SIM when they regain mobile phone service. Furthermore, now mobile operators allow subscribers to buy up to three SIMs, taking into consideration the need to restrict the amount of SIMs purchased while also recognizing that most Guineans do so not for criminal activities but to sponsor their rural kin who may not be able to register, or for their children below the age of eighteen.

Despite the efforts of operators, important shortcomings linked with SIM registration remain. First, SIM registration complicates the much-lauded developmental influence of mobile phones as it represents a shift towards erecting barriers to access. Such requirements present important access difficulties to the most vulnerable populations. Second, there are no robust empirical studies proving that these regulations make a difference in terms of crime detection as criminals can circumvent the rules. A survey of Organization for Economic Cooperation and Development (OECD) member countries found little evidence that criminals would be affected. Canada's privacy commissioner rejected the notion upon investigation as well as the Czech Republic, Greece, Ireland, the Netherlands and Poland. In Africa, reasons to doubt the effectiveness of SIM registration for apprehending criminals are even more relevant as the policies assume that SIM cards are reducible to one user. Yet, as aforementioned, the difficulty of registration and the weakness of national identification infrastructure in countries such as Guinea has induced operators and governments to allow proxies to register SIM cards. Accordingly, it is common for registration data not to reflect the future user of a SIM card. Finally, SIM registration makes subscribers wary of breaches in privacy. For example, the VidaNET program in Mexico provides a treatment reminder system to those with HIV and has faced challenges as users fear that SIM registration has jeopardized their medical confidentiality.[118]

As of 1999, no country in Africa had data privacy legislation.[119] To this day, implementation and enforcement capacity remain limited as well as worrisome. Although surveillance is part of modernity and often even desirable, the way in which SIM registration has been implemented often lacks appropriate consultation, transparency and fair privacy laws. SIM registration reduces the anonymity once afforded by prepaid airtime. While it supposedly helps government track terrorists and allows mobile operators to better tailor their offers to the needs of subscribers, the implementation of such laws also raises concerns about the right to privacy of subscribers and the extent of subscriber data shared by operators with the government. For example, in the recent ambush which led to the death of four US soldiers in Niger, the operation was launched after intelligence officials had intercepted a signal from the cellphone of a terrorist.[120] This means that subscriber identity is readily available and can even be shared with foreign powers. The SIM registration process in Guinea faces these overarching privacy concerns, as well as more locally relevant difficulties which have led operators to further acculturate the technology to local needs.

Certain MTN-agents complain that Axon takes up too much memory space, others are temporarily denied access to the platform due to password errors, and overall many 'want to apply their logic to the application, not understanding that it already has its own'.[121] Sales coordinators at MTN are each responsible for a different neighborhood or locality and for guiding FS and POS on how to use Axon (see photo 18). In Conakry, daily sales coordinators must check-in to the MTN headquarters, despite the fact that many live in the neighborhood assigned to them, before driving out to each POS or FS unit in their designated locality to collect the earnings of the previous day. It often takes the sales coordinator in charge of Ratoma, a neighborhood 22 miles away from MTN-headquarters, around three hours to reach his destination.[122]

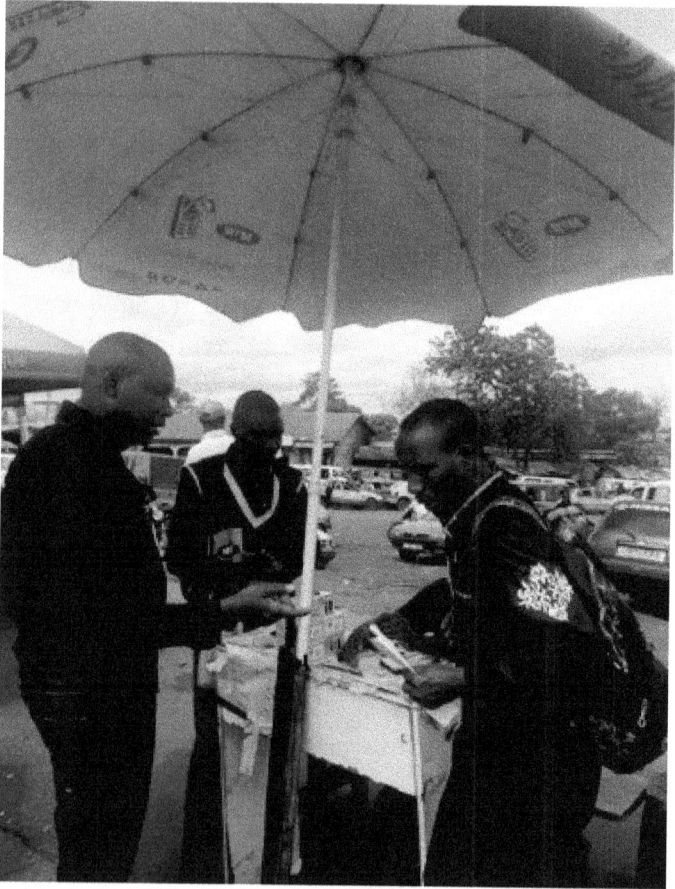

Photo 18. Sales coordinator Ba checking on a POS in Ratoma, Conakry

This is time wasted for the Ratoma sales coordinator, Ibrahima Ba, considering that he lives in the neighborhood and left it earlier that morning to clock-in at the MTN headquarters. Once at MTN-headquarters he calls the FS and POS under his supervision to ask if they are encountering any difficulties, the answer is invariably 'no'. Yet, when Ba arrives in Ratoma he finds FS selling faulty SIMs, struggling to sell credit, and to use the Axon app, or even POS which have closed and are now occupied by 'Mamas' selling their products under the MTN emblem which needs to be repainted to safeguard the brand's prestige. The lack of trust between the sales coordinator and his units reveals the limits of mobile phones, or virtual communications. In the same vein, despite the advent of mobile money, each day Ba stops to collect the profit made by his units, bundles of cash are thus exchanged on the sidewalk in plain sight and brought back to MTN headquarters at the end of the day. Acknowledging the shortcomings of the process, MTN recently sought to facilitate it by using mobile phones.

Since the start of 2018, MTN has been subcontracting a company that oversees the transfer of SIM registration earnings by mobile money. Sales coordinators can now focus their attention primarily on creating new POS and ensuring the visibility of the brand, rather than physically transporting earnings from their assigned neighborhood to headquarters. Nonetheless, they continue to roam around the city to reassure FS and POS that they are valued and to oversee the well-functioning of their operations. The SIM registration system must not only be acculturated to the needs of the customers but also to the ways of MTN-agents and the local context in which they operate. Overall, it is evident that operators created these chains of credit distribution and SIM registration with Guinean realities in mind, understanding that for the pre-paid system to work, a vast number of call-boxers, POS, and Foot Soldiers is needed. Over time, however, the system of acquiring credit and SIM registration has not only restructured the departments of mobile operators but has built on and re-shaped the daily habits of Guineans. Mobile operators are constantly engaging in a tug of war or 'game of mirrors' with subscribers to bridge global and local cultures while shaping consumer appropriation so their company can profit from it.

## F. Oral Traditions and Customer Loyalty

In Guinea, as in most other West African countries, there is a hyper-presence of mobile telephony marketing. Streets are filled with advertising signs of all sizes, call-boxes, Points of Sale, and umbrellas with the colors of the different operators. The Marketing, Customer Relations, and Sales and Distribution departments at MTN work together to institute marketing strategies – including various forms of community engagement and bonus offers – in touch with local trends while also being profitable to the company. Amongst these trends, MTN recognizes the role of mobile phones as a modern vector to maintain oral traditions. In villages it was customary to greet all of one's neighbors after getting up in the morning. Nowadays, urban dwellers can call their rural kin for greetings, virtually bridging the rural-urban 'divide' and upholding the importance of spoken word. As the CEO of MTN points out, time spent on 'greetings during telecommunications often generates more revenue than the conversation itself'.[123] Sometimes exchanging greetings and incurring about a friend's health and that of their family is even the sole purpose of the call.

The vast majority of Guineans prefer to call rather than to send SMS messages. For mobile operators, 85% of revenue is generated from voice, 9.2% from data, and 2 % from SMS, and most will not leave a voicemail. Leaving a voicemail is not a common practice in most West African nations as it entails speaking to a machine and, aside from the youth, many do not know how to access their voicemail – which reveals a common lack of digital literacy amongst adults. Users also prefer calling to sending an SMS. Low rates of SMS in countries like Guinea, can be explained by the fact that more than half of the population is estimated to be illiterate. However, even for those who can write, typing text messages on standard phones can be strenuous and, assuming that their correspondent is in a zone with enough mobile phone service to receive the message, there is no guarantee that they will distinguish it from the incessant SMS advertisements sent by mobile operators. The caller would rather call again to ensure that his message is heard and not relinquish prized human interaction. Mobile phones are building on and accelerating pre-existing social relations and norms.[124] With regards to these norms, and the cautionary nature of Guineans towards companies, corporations and the government, MTN agents often directly visit the homes of subscribers. These agents, known as members of 'Team Frontline', offer gadgets, pens, t-shirts and sometimes also low-cost smartphones to subscribers with standard mobile phones, increasing both revenue for the company from internet data and loyalty from their subscribers.[125] Nonetheless, mobile phones are also altering these norms of face-to-face interaction and the culture of orality as shown in the steady decline of 'voice' communications for internet data in Guinea and throughout the sub-Saharan region. Two-thirds of mobile phone users south of the Sahara are categorized as 'talkers', meaning that they primarily use their mobile devices for traditional voice and messaging services.[126] Many older subscribers, above the age of 40 years old, and non-smartphone users fall into that category. Trends, however, show a rapid transition towards higher levels of engagement underpinned by increased accessibility to mobile data services, smartphones, and youth who almost exclusively rely on mobile phones to surf the internet.

Human interactions between agents of mobile operators and subscribers often foster a strong sense of loyalty. Loyalty comes with high standards of accountability, as subscribers often hold the brand responsible for their successes and failures in life. For example, many subscribers believe that mobile operators influence the results of their children on national exams since they can now receive the outcome by text-message. The 'Team Outbound' is a branch of the Customer relations department which calls subscribers to collect feedback following a complaint, a visit from an agent or an initiative by MTN.[127] The agents of the 'Team Outbound' are all in their early twenties and have degrees in journalism, marketing, management and other spheres but have fallen back on this job until they find a better opportunity. In a day, these agents emit between 150-200 calls, usually reaching around 80 subscribers, altering from speaking Soussou, Poular, Malinké, French and sometimes English depending on the caller. On the day of results for the 6th grade national exam, a subscriber gave MTN a 9/10 on a satisfaction scale because his child had earned 9th place on the exam while another gave a 5/10 since his child had failed the exam.[128] Others were satisfied but could not give a 10/10 because 'only God deserves such distinction', so they preferred to give a 'strong' 9/10. Considering that most customer care agents speak all three national languages and French, it is clear that such subscriber responses are not a result of misunderstandings caused by a language barrier, but rather are representative of the degree to which mobile operators have shaped and have become entrenched in people's lives.

## G. Community Engagement and Growth-Inducing Services of Mobile Operators

Mobile operators are heavily engaged in community service, and since 2017 MTN has collaborated with the Guinean Ministry of Education and the West Africa Progress Initiative (WAPI) to sponsor an annual sporting event in schools.[129] It was the first time since 1977 that sports returned to the school sector, and the initiative was lauded by the public as well as by the Ministry of Sports and Pre-University Education. Mobile operators also work closely with the government to modernize regulatory conditions in mobile-enabled solutions. Each year the MTN Y'ello care programs throughout sub-Saharan Africa dedicate 21 days to actively investing in education, the digitalization of teaching and raising awareness (see photo 19). In Guinea, MTN's Y'ello care program was first implemented five years ago. In 2017, MTN workers in Conakry raised funds and volunteered their time to clean out a space in a building known for organizing school events, known as 'the House of the Youth', and to provide it with computers and internet connection.[130] In other countries south of the Sahara, Y'ello care has led to the creation of robotics and coding camps in Swaziland; the laying out of fiber to enable school connectivity in Kenya; sessions on digital literacy for 260 women vendors in Ivory Coast; and in Cameroon, MTN staff constructed a multi-purpose building to enhance the enrollment capacity of an institution educating deaf children.[131]

Along with integrating mobile technologies in schools to enable access to greater learning opportunities, mobile operators in Guinea have recently introduced mobile money services. Mobile money, known as 'MoMo', is meant to reduce poverty and inequality by increasing financial inclusion. MTN launched MoMo in 2014 but Mobile Financial Services (MFS) did not become a stand-alone department until 2016. The department now accounts for a registered mobile money customer base of approximately 1.7 million – 60,000 of which are active users, in a country where only 5% of the population has a bank account.[132] Nonetheless, mobile money is still in its implementation stages in Guinea, and services such as the payment of electricity bills through MoMo are not yet as available as they are in Cameroon and other West African nations.

Photo 19. MTN Y'ello care poster promoting its permanent
theme of 'investing in education for all'

The most advanced adoption of mobile money services is in
East Africa. M-Pesa, 'M' for mobile and 'Pesa' for money in
Swahili, was launched in 2007 and now has over 30 million users
across ten East African countries. Kenya alone accounts for 18
million users which represents about 38% of the country's 48
million people.[133] In December 2016, 614 million M-Pesa
transactions were processed and 6 billion overall were processed
during the year which amounts to 529 per second. In Africa,
around 80% of the population lacks access to formal banking
services and poor infrastructure often hamper access to banks
and ATMs.[134] MoMo services have brought an alternative to
these shortcomings. Yet, while in China and India MoMo
services were integrated to flourish with the traditional banking
sector, in Africa MoMo services deployed by many operators

function separately from and are often in competition with banks. This can be problematic as without the support of banks there is no cash and MoMo is no more than virtual currency. Many Guineans are wary of this virtual currency, just like they were cautious at the onset of mobile internet, which was perceived as a way for the government to spy on the population. Suspicious of change instituted from authorities, many prefer to 'first look to the neighbor to see if it works'.[135]

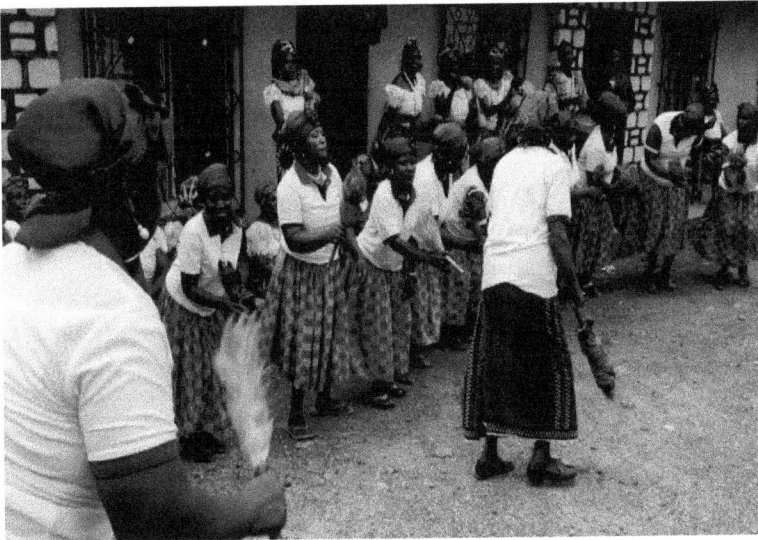

Photo 20. A 'tontine' in Bamenda, Cameroon

The adoption of MoMo by the Guinean population has also been slowed by drawbacks. Fraudsters extract money after acquiring the MoMo password of subscribers and MoMo users often encounter technological malfunctions like the non-reception of a notification following the completion of a transaction. To instill trust and develop electronic banking, mobile operators have primarily targeted the agricultural sector, but they also collaborate with traditional microfinance groups, locally known as 'serré' in Soussou or 'tontine' in French (see photo 20). Mobile phone based lending has increased with the advent of organizations such as 'First Access', which help women in African nations build financial identities through their mobile data. First Access turns prepaid mobile records into personal financial profiles for people without bank accounts. In a region of the world where women are much less likely than men to have home ownership papers, land titles, bank accounts and other official documents, First Access allows women to lend or borrow money by providing access to instant mobile credit scores to loan officers and other lending committees.[136] In Guinea, MTN is looking to capitalize on the extreme popularity of lottery and betting companies by partnering with Guinée Games and Guinée des Jeux to permit the purchase of lottery tickets and the payment of lottery gains via mobile money. Through such acculturation of mobile banking, MoMo is increasingly becoming an integral part of the Guinean landscape and re-shaping the habits of the population. Currently, students are the ones predominantly using mobile money, as they are the most technologically savvy and understand the advantages that come along with the service. More generally, the youth are the trend-setters in the telecommunication sector.

## H. 'MTN-Cool' and the Value of the Youth

The primary target population for mobile operators in Guinea, like most West African nations, is the youth (see photo 21). According to the most recent estimates, 40% of the population in Africa is below the age of fifteen years old with an additional 19% between fifteen and twenty-four years old, amounting to approximately three-fifths of the overall

Photo 21. Youth playing soccer in Conakry

population below the age of twenty-five. West and Central Africa are the youngest regions with respectively 43% and 46% of people below the age of fifteen (Smith 2018: 19 and 32). Guinea falls within the norm in West Africa with over 60% of the population below the age of twenty-four. The importance of young adults – primarily between ages fifteen and twenty-four – for mobile operators lies as much in the revenue they generate as in their role as 'the intermediate link between the younger siblings and parents'.[137] Through their activity on social media and word of mouth, the youth, and particularly students, act as leaders of opinion and are the promoters of mobile telephony. Aside from the youth, a few times a year all MTN employees leave the headquarters in Conakry to promote the brand throughout the city. The objective, similar to 'Road Shows', is to appeal to the mass market with music, small gifts and other activities. Aside from such large-scale promotional events, mobile operators tailor their offers and bonus bundles to specific populations, such as the 'M'Ma Boss' offer for High Value Customers and companies which generate a lot of revenue.

Bonus bundles vary based on location and the time of the year. For example, MTN offers more bonus bundles in Location Area Refill (LAR) such as inland rural localities which tend to generate less revenue than city dwellers. Mobile operators also offer special bundles on market days and increase their bonus offers during the rainy season, as road conditions further deteriorate and subscribers are less likely to access a POS to purchase credit. Bonus bundles are also tailored to special holidays, such as MTN's religion-based quizzes by SMS throughout the month of Ramadan. These SMS quizzes are an effort to make up for losses in revenue during Ramadan as Guineans, approximately 85% of whom are Muslims, are engaging in pious activities.[138] Along with the SMS quiz Ramadan promotion, Guineans can subscribe to similar bundles and listen to Qur'anic verses, hear stories based on the life of the Prophet, follow the call to Mecca, and find out what to do and

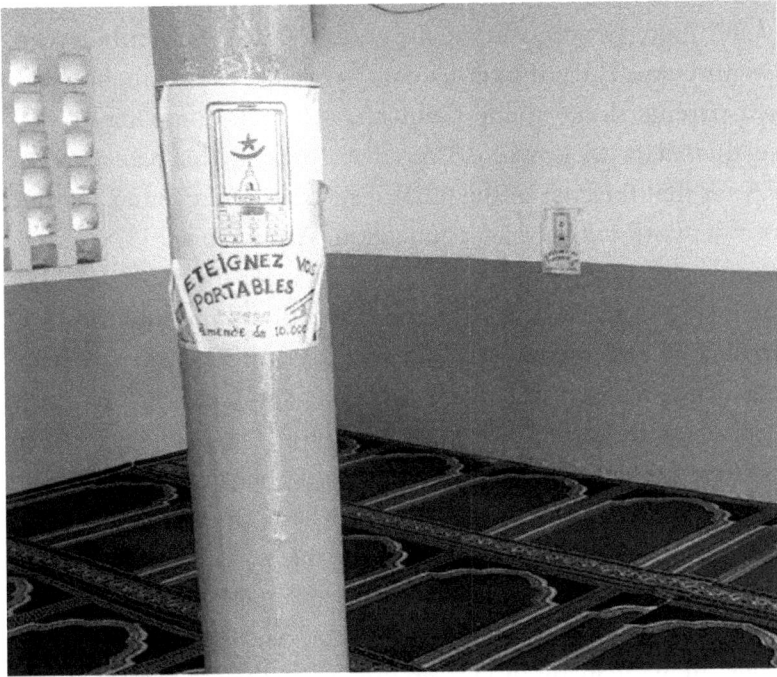

Photo 22. Signs in a mosque in Conakry asking to switch off phones

not to do during Ramadan.[139] Mobile phones can also disrupt religious practices and have become so popular that in certain mosques there are signs reminding people to shut off their mobile phone or incur a fine (see photo 22). Yet, in mosques and churches followers often refuse to switch off their devices and prayers are interrupted by ringtones. For many, even in pious settings, turning off their mobile phones is like 'being asked to switch off one's ambition for prestige and social status' (Nyamnjoh 2009: 4).

Despite the popularity of religion based quizzes and bonuses, amongst MTN's various offers 'MTN Cool' is the company's most popular cellphone plan. 'MTN Cool' mainly attracts the youth and is a prime example of corporate acculturation as a form of mutual and reciprocal process between consumers and operators. Guineans can subscribe to

'MTN Cool' daily and call for 3 GNF/sec, instead of the usual 9 GNF/sec, between midnight and 6:00 am. Subscribers can also purchase 1GB of internet data to use during the night.[140] As their parents sleep, young Guineans call their companions and use their data to download movies. At first, the plan was so popular that the cost of the traffic exceeded the revenue and the busy network led to slow connection. As a result, MTN raised the internet tariff from 3,000 GNF a night to 10,000 GNF. There were around 3,000 internet subscribers the night before the change and only about 160 remained the following day, a 95% loss in subscribers.[141] MTN responded by recently introducing the offer 'Gouli', meaning 'twin' in Soussou, which doubles the internet volume bought on each purchase (1 GB purchased, 2 GB received). At the onset of mobile telephony, operators often named their offers in ways that weren't linked to the local *lingua franca* or in touch with realities. For example, in Cameroon the population renamed the first bonus 'Jack Bauer', drawing inspiration from the protagonist in the TV series '24 hours' who endlessly makes calls throughout the film. Nowadays, mobile operators name their offers, like 'Gouli', to be in touch with societal happenings, the slang of the youth, and appeal to less educated populations. In 2017, MTN-Cameroon launched the 'Je Wanda' bonus which means 'I am surprised' in Camfranglais, a language of expression primarily used by the youth mixing French, English and local languages. Even though MTN advertises 'Gouli' as part of the 'MTN-Cool' plan, this new internet bonus can be used at any time of the day, as not to overload the bandwidth. Despite its local branding, the MTN Customer Relations department soon received complaints from young Guineans wishing to revert to hourly plans rather than larger volume offers as to better manage spending based on immediate needs.[142]

The 'MTN Cool' plan exemplifies how the Marketing, Customer Relations and Sales and Distribution departments work together to first identify local trends (i.e. the youth prefer to call or surf the net in the privacy of the night); tailor the company's offers and rates based on the target population; and, in turn, effectively enhance existing habits to generate revenue. Such marketing decisions have the power to (re)-shape the rhythm of life in Guinea, as a large segment of the population remains awake at night. Offers like 'MTN Cool' portray the dynamic process of corporate acculturation in the sphere of 'glocalization'. MTN is adapting the use of a foreign technology – mobile telephony – to cultural traits and social patterns in Guinea and sets the field for subscribers to appropriate the technology. However, as demonstrated by the case of 'SIM Box' frauds, Guineans exercise agency outside of the boundaries set by operators, leading the latter to re-consider their operations and even form new units in their departments. Whereas assimilation suggests that one group becomes increasingly like the other, the transformations taking place in Guinea are clearly multilateral, as both mobile operators and subscribers shape each other in a constant 'game of mirrors'.

## Notes

91    Maggie Fick and Joseph Cotterill. 'MTN: What next for Africa's $17bn Telecoms Group?' *Financial Times*, 14 Mar. 2017.

92    The list was culled from over 11,000 brand mentions cited through a mobile survey by consumers in 19 African countries, who collectively represent 74% of the continent's population. Abdi Latif Dahir. 'Africa's Top Brands Are Losing out at Home to International Rivals as an Economic Downturn Bites.' *Quartz*, 6 Mar. 2017; 'MTN Group 2016 Tax Report'. *Mtn.com*, 2016.

93    'MTN Group 2016 Tax Report'. *Mtn.com*, 2016.

94    For the sake of comparison, with 10,000 GNF ($1.10) one can eat a plate of rice and fish on street-side joints.

95   The Guinean population is estimated to be around 11 million people. 'ARPT: Autorité de régulation des postes et télécommunication, rapport 2ème trimeste 2017'. *ARPT*, 2017, 1.

96   On the Human Development Index in 2015, Guinea ranked 183 out of 188 countries, while Cameroon ranked 153. 'Guinea.' *Human Development Report 2016*, UNDP, 2016; 'Cameroon'. *Human Development Report 2016*, UNDP, 2016.

97 Interview with Papa Sow in Conakry, CEO of MTN-Guinea, 06/20/17

98 Interview with Reuben Opata in Conakry, Director of Information Technology at MTN-Guinea, 06/18/17

99   'ARPT: Autorité de régulation des postes et télécommunication, rapport 2ème trimeste 2017'. 2017, 8.

100 'Guinea Population'. *Worldometers*, 2018. Accessed February 6th, 2018.

101   Dina Spector. 'What Is WiMax? And How Does It Work?' *Business Insider*, 23 Sept. 2010.

102 ARPT: Autorité de régulation des postes et télécommunication, rapport 2ème trimeste 2017.' 2017, 5.

103 'Même les personnes qui sont de la classe supérieure préfèrent être pré-payés, car il existe cette notion de dire « je ne sais pas de quoi demain sera fait » donc ils préfèrent acheter se dont ils ont besoin maintenant que de prendre un forfait qui les engages dans le long terme'. Interview with Papa Sow in Conakry, CEO of MTN-Guinea, 06/20/17

104 A POS or a call-box, is a box big enough for a person to stand in it made of timber with plywood on the lower half and with four windows that open outwards, is often not a defined structure or a store but can  refer to a person on the street with a small advertising sign from a mobile operator indicating that he sells cellphone credit.

105 Interview and field research with Ibrahima Ba in Ratoma, Conakry, Sales coordinator at MTN-Guinea, 06/10/17

106 Interview and field research with Lawrence Ngalah in Kindia, Head of Sales and Distribution at MTN-Guinea, 06/14/17

107 Kevin Donovan and Aaron Martin. 'The Rise of African SIM Registration: Mobility, Identity, Surveillance and Resistance.' *SSRN Electronic Journal* (2012).

108 Foot Soldiers earn a commission of 1,000 GNF on each 3,000 GNF SIM that they sell after the first call is made by the customer.

109 Interview and field research with Ibrahima Ba in Ratoma, Conakry, Sales coordinator at MTN-Guinea, 06/10/17

110 'ICSS Making Substantial Progress in Fighting Fraud'. *International Carrier Sales & Solutions (ICSS)*, 1 Aug. 2012.

111 David Emery. 'Beware of Calls from These 'Killer Phone Numbers''. *ThoughtCo*, 9 Apr. 2018.

112 Ibid.

113 Anandita Singh Mankotia. 'Make Biometric Proof Must to Buy Sim Card: Delhi Police Commissioner | Gadgets Now'. *Gadget Now*, 21 June 2013; Maggie Fick and Joseph Cotterill. 'MTN: What next for Africa's $17bn Telecoms Group?' *Financial Times*, 14 Mar. 2017.

114 As a result of failing to heed this order, in 2015 MTN was fined $5.2 billion before settling on $1.7 billion. Fick, 'MTN: What next for Africa's', *Financial Times*, 14 Mar. 2017.

115 Ibid.

116 Interview with Reuben Opata in Conakry, Director of Information Technology at MTN-Guinea, 06/18/17

117 Donovan and Martin. 'The Rise of African SIM Registration', *SSRN Electronic Journal*, 2012.

118 David Banisar. 'Privacy and data protection around the world', *Proceedings of the 21st International Conference on Privacy and Personal Data Protection*, 1999.

119 Ibid.

120 Eric Schmitt and Rukmini Callimachi. 'Niger Ambush Suspect May Be in Custody, Officials Say'. *The New York Times*, The New York Times, 16 Apr. 2018.

121 Interview and field research with Lawrence Ngalah in Kindia, Head of Sales and Distribution at MTN-Guinea, 06/14/17

122 Interview and field research with Ibrahima Ba in Ratoma, Conakry, Sales coordinator at MTN-Guinea, 06/10/17

123 'En Occident on appel quand on a quelque chose à régler puis on avance, ici le téléphone remplace la tradition orale ou rien que les salutations génèrent plus de revenus que ce que les gens disent'. Interview with Papa Sow in Conakry, CEO of MTN-Guinea, 06/20/17

124 'Guinée: opérateurs télécoms, une hausse de 11% des revenus au premier trimestre'. *Guinee360.com*, 18 Aug. 2016. Accessed February 11th, 2018.

125 Interview with Mariama Djéllo Diallo in Conakry, Head of Customer Relations at MTN-Guinea, 06/10/17

126 GSMA. *The Mobile Economy – sub-Saharan Africa, 2017*, 3.

127 To reduce costs, MTN externalized the Customer Relations department and since January 2018 the 'Team Outbound' has been moved to Dakar, Senegal. Subscribers now voice their concerns and satisfactions to Guinean students and residents living in Dakar.

128 Observation at Customer Relations, Headquarters of MTN-Guinea in Conakry, 06/10/17

129 'Sport fin du tournoi SMUS sponsorisé par MTN Guinée...' *Africaguinee.com - Site Officiel d'informations sur la Guinée et l'Afrique*, 3 May 2017.

130 Oumar Diallo. 'Guinée: MTN lance son programme d'assistance sociale "Y'ello Care' actualité de la Guinée'. *Aminata*, Aminata.com les nouvelles de la république de Guinée, 10 June 2017.

131 These Y'ello care initiatives, found on the MTN group website, took place in 2016. 'Y'ello Care'. *MTN Group*.

132 Interview with Okwaro Jeremiah in Conakry, Head of Mobile Financial Services at MTN-Guinea, 06/11/17

133 Kieron Monks. 'M-Pesa: Kenya's Mobile Success Story Turns 10'. *CNN*, Cable News Network, 24 Feb. 2017.

134 Alex Alexander et al. 'How Fintech Is Reaching the Poor in Africa and Asia: a Start-up Perspective'. *World Bank Group*, Mar. 2017.

135 Interview with Okwaro Jeremiah, Head of Mobile Financial Services at MTN-Guinea, 06/11/17

136 John Aglionby. 'Financial Times Fintech Takes off in Africa as Lenders Tap Mobile Technology'. *Financial Times*, 16 May 2016.

137 Interview with Lalla Cheriff in Conakry, Manager of Brand and Communication at MTN-Guinea, 06/10/17. 'Population Pyramid of Guinea'. *PopulationPyramid.net*. Accessed February 6th, 2018.

138 'M'Ma Boss' means 'My Boss'. An example of a quiz question would be 'in what year was the prophet Muhammad born?', it costs 200 GNF ($0.022) to participate in the quiz and each week the winner receives a 2 million GNF ($220) gift-card. Some MTN employees explain the decrease in revenue during Ramadan to less calls made to lovers and time spent in bars, as Guineans devote a larger part of their day to praying and abiding by the precepts of the Quran.

139 'MTNGuinée: Promo Ramadan 2015'. *Africaguinee.com*, 22 June 2015. Accessed February 10th, 2018.

140 Guineans subscribe to MTN Cool by entering *100*6# for credit and *100*3# for internet data.

141 Interview with Amadou Oury Diallo in Conakry, Agent of Data and Devices Management at MTN-Guinea, 06/11/17

142 Interview with Mariama Djéllo Diallo in Conakry, Head of Customer Relations at MTN-Guinea, 06/10/17

# Chapter 4

## ICT4D and Ungrounded Optimism

### A. Mobile Phones for Development: Africa's Success Story

Times have changed since Manuel Castells wrote, at the turn of the millennium, about 'Africa's technological apartheid at the dawn of the information age' (Castells 2000: 92). With an estimated 420 million unique mobile subscribers in 2016 – second only to Asia – and the fastest growing mobile penetration rate in the world, sub-Saharan Africa is no longer excluded from the digital age or a 'black hole' of informational capitalism.[143] In the two years leading up to 2016, smartphone connections doubled to nearly 200 million – accounting for a quarter of mobile connections – and mobile internet penetration continues to increase across the continent. West Africa is predicted to experience a rise of internet penetration from 30% to 43% by 2020.[144] As a result of the region's unprecedented demographic growth, which saw the population south of the Sahara quadruple from 230 million in 1960 to 1 billion in 2015, it is expected that by 2020 the region will have more than half a billion mobile unique subscribers (Smith 2018: 2).

The rapid appropriation of the technology by Africans and reduction in barriers to mobile connectivity since the turn of the century are largely attributed to market liberalization and privatization, the availability of low-cost handsets, and business-marketing decisions made by mobile operators to lower the cost of access with offers such as bonuses and prepaid airtime.[145] Bonus offers like 'MTN Cool' in Guinea display how society and technology are interdependent through the inner workings of cultural and social appropriation (consumers) and acculturation (operators.) The rate of mobile subscriptions is set to increase as mobile operators continue to tailor their marketing strategies and offers to underserved groups, specifically women and the youth, encouraging them to uptake mobile services. In 2016, women south of the Sahara were 17% less likely than men to own a mobile phone and less than a fifth of under-16-year-olds had a mobile subscription.[146] The youth will increasingly be the primary drivers of subscriber growth in the future as the region has the highest rate of population growth in the world. The United Nations predicts that by 2050 sub-Saharan Africa will be home to 2 billion people, accounting for approximately 25% of the global population.[147] By then Europe is expected to have a smaller population than in 2015. This simultaneous demographic boom and 'mobile revolution' occurring south of the Sahara has given rise to grandiloquent predictions for the region's future.

The growing ICT4D literature emerging from Africa basks in 'Afro-optimism'. The literature overwhelmingly praises the soaring rise of mobile phones for their capacity to 'lift' the continent out of poverty and aligns itself with Jeffrey Sachs' claim that 'mobile phones are the single most transformative technology for development' (Carmody 2012: 1). In 2016, mobile technologies and services generated $110 billion of economic value south of the Sahara – nearing 8% of the region's GDP – and contributed $13 billion in taxes to the state coffers. The mobile sector ecosystem also supported approximately 3.5 million jobs in the region, which is most likely an underestimation in light of the importance of the informal cellular economy and the impossibility of tracking the number of street vendors or mobile phone traders and repairers like Proxy and Willy (Chapter 2). The entrepreneurial opportunities generated by the rise of the informal cellular economy and second-hand phone market constitute another lauded benefit from the spread of mobile phones, as best exemplified by the pervasive 'Call-Box system' in West Africa. Furthermore, youth are driving the appropriation of smart mobile devices and the creation of mobile-based innovation, as explored in the case of app-developers in Buea. They have already made a significant impact in the fields of health (M-Pedigree), commerce (M-Pesa), and education (OkpaBac). Investment in the tech start-up ecosystem is growing, as some 77 tech start-ups in the region raised $367 million in seed money in 2016, a 33% increase from the previous year.[148] Modernity-inducing mobile innovations in West Africa are not exclusive of tradition and often serve to uphold established cultural practices, as exemplified by the creation of the mobile application 'Heritage' to teach African languages to young urbanites or children in the diaspora. Likewise, the networks for 'distance healing' by tradi-practitioners have now grown internationally, and the democratization of mobile telephony has not only facilitated but also reshaped the healing process – effectively compounding change and continuity.

Through such innovations and 'creative' forms of appropriation, new ICTs like mobile phones are widely believed to enable economic 'catch-up' through technological leapfrogging. ICTs are viewed as 'time portals' that will undoubtedly bring modernity to the populations of the developing world (Carmody 2012: 2). Amongst the pillars of modernity, mobile phones are thought to help promote democracy and active citizenship, whether through the creation of large WhatsApp groups, virtual political parties like 'Le Cameroun C'est Le Cameroun', or through the delivery of voter education (Aker 2011). In such cases, as well as in business and healthcare, the emphasis is put on the potential of mobile phones to enhance socioeconomic development by facilitating the circulation of 'useful information' (Arachambault 2017: 3). For example, in the district of Nyakokombo in Cameroon cocoa farmers now have better access to market prices and can increase their profits. Mobile phones also reduce price dispersion, cutting out middlemen and permitting producers to earn more for their labor. They also lead to more efficient arbitrage between different spatial markets, which is particularly relevant for international networks such as the export of grey parrots with red hearts from Nyakokombo to Europe. As such, the mobile phone has become both an index of modernization as well as a driver of development.[149]

Given the transformative potential of mobile phones, the 'digital divide' is particularly problematic and one that should be urgently bridged to guarantee access to the technology for all. In doing so, West African populations would emerge from the 'mobile margins' – which are social spaces created on the margins of the state – and be connected with the possibilities of a globalized world (De Bruijn 2008: 4). Rural dwellers are thought to benefit the most from such a transformation and, as shown in the case of Guinea, are a prime target population for mobile operators. Even with the increased formality of the SIM registration process, subscribers can still purchase up to 3 SIMs and sponsor their rural kin. Furthermore, MTN adopted the use of the Axon platform for its 'Foot Soldiers' to facilitate the activation of SIMs in remote areas with limited mobile service. Overall, with the capital Conakry being saturated, mobile operators in Guinea have made specific efforts to increasingly tailor their marketing strategies to the needs of rural populations. By increasing access to mobile phones in rural areas, and, in turn, to services such as mobile money, mobile operators are bridging the 'rural-urban' divide where governments have yet to build enough roads and other infrastructure to do so. In considering all of these factors, mobile phones are largely presented as a silver bullet or panacea for the troubles of sub-Saharan Africa and will help 'save' the region.

The above-mentioned advantages derived from the local appropriation and acculturation of mobile phones – i.e. the 'glocalization' of the technology – are undeniable and welcomed. However, the ICT4D narrative rests on a teleological model of ascendant stages of development with 'backward' developing nations that do not match the realities of West Africa and the wider sub-Saharan region. Furthermore, such a discourse is predicated on a generic view of poverty in which technological solutions are prescribed for problem construed as technical hurdles. This discourse displays a striking lack of nuance in its propensity to associate mobile phone access with development-inducing functions. While ICTs, particularly the Internet, offer digital channels that can deliver informational and communicative power – the mere uptake of ICTs does not lead 'to innovation by virtue of the technological capacities of the device' (Nyamnjoh et al. 2016: 5). 'Transplanting' digital technologies is not enough to yield positive results – mobile phones provide a mean for empowerment but are not synonymous to progress. Like older media and technologies that hold the potential to educate and modernize Africa, such as the radio, television, popular theater and mobile cinema, the spread of mobile phones has yielded mixed results. At the outset, few predicted that mobile telephony would leapfrog the landline stage disseminate as rapidly as it has south of the Sahara. This probably accounts for the tendency to identify mobile phones as 'Africa's big success story' of the early 21$^{st}$ century (Butler 2005). However, mobile telephony being a technology bereft of intrinsic agency, the question remains what – positive or negative – outcomes the users of cellphones south of the Sahara will bring about. It could be better education as well as more pornography.

## B. 'Saving Africa' and Overloading Mobile Expectations

In West Africa, development induced by mobile phones is still more of an expectation than a reality (De Bruijn 2009: 13). As demonstrated by the case studies of Cameroon and Guinea, mobile phones have been absorbed into economic structures in West Africa through appropriation and acculturation. Yet, there is no indication that they have transformed them to yield better macro-economic results at the national level. This analysis rings true at the scale of the sub-Saharan region as a whole and pushes back against the ICT4D literature, which suffers from an intellectual disarticulation between the successful spread of mobile telephony and its supposed impacts (Murphy and Carmody 2015: 211). According to the 2016 World Bank World Development report, despite the rapid spread of mobile phones across the globe, digital dividends – the broader development benefits from using these technologies – have 'lagged behind'.[150] Greater digital adoption is not by itself enough for the benefits of mobile telephony to be evenly distributed. Rather the World Bank advocates strengthened regulations that ensure competition among businesses, adapting the skills of workers to the demands of the new economy, and ensuring that institutions are accountable. In doing so, it addresses the shortcomings of most West African governments in providing adequate infrastructure and regulations. These failings did not impede the rapid spread of mobile telephony. Instead they often allowed less risk-adverse operators with rapidly deployable networks to make quick returns on investments, but they are not conducive to the long-term investments required to build modern, networked economies.[151]

The rapid spread of mobile telephony in sub-Saharan Africa is primarily due to the fact that it is an 'inverse infrastructure' that is largely self-organizing and requires smaller investments than for landlines, roads or electrical grids (Carmody 2012: 8). On the supply side, the dissemination of mobile phones has been facilitated by agency exercised within the informal cellular economy and the failure of the state to provide adequate infrastructure delivery for landlines. Mobile phones have contributed to the growth of the informal sector through employment creation, which is favorable in terms of livelihoods but can be problematic in terms of longer development impacts. The agency displayed in the informal sector – such as Avenue Kennedy in Yaoundé – is a source of employment, but the success of the informal trading and repairing economy is largely reliant on the downward cycle of selling cheap low-quality phones, which break down and as such require tinkering from phone repairers. Mobile phones provide greater access to information and communications, and they have significant poverty-reduction benefits and potentialities, but their link with development in sub-Saharan Africa remains largely putative and overestimated (Arachambault 2017: 11).

The data released by the mobile industry in sub-Saharan Africa appears very promising but it often conceals a less glossy reality at a second glance. For example, while the mobile phone industry has created 3.5 million jobs south of the Sahara, most are low-profit and low-productivity activities such as those of call-boxers. In Cameroon, call-boxers only earn 5% of the credit they sell and often make more from selling whisky sachets and cigarettes than credit. The efficiency of the credit distribution chain in rural areas, such as in Nyakokombo, is at the very least doubtful, given that the provision of credit can depend on the comings and goings of the 'trusted motorcycle taxi man' who delivers bread to the village. While celebrating local agency and resilience in the 'glocalization' of mobile phones, we cannot ignore the deeper structural problems at the risk of overstating the ability of mobile phones to solve them. The bread taxi-man and solar panels are creative appropriations, but they do not resolve the entrenched shortcomings in terms of access to resources, opportunities and basic infrastructure that are far more deeply entrenched than the digital divide in West Africa (Arachambault 2017: 40). Similarly, surging rates of mobile penetration in West Africa and the use of mobile phones to reform commerce have improved connection to the 'global economy', but the majority of calls in Ghana, for example, are not for business but 'used to maintain family relations' (Slater and Kwami 2005). As such, mobile phones are primarily socially connecting rather than economically beneficial to global production chains. Even when they have helped improve commercial efficiency, such as in the case of cocoa, fish and parrot traders in Nyakokombo, mobile phones are often not exploited to their full capacity. For example, parrot capturers sell their preys for 12,000 CFA ($21) trusting the middleman that grey parrots are sold for 100,000 CFA ($181) in Europe. A quick search on the internet would show them that in reality the price of a grey parrot is on average around 600,000 CFA ($1,060).

Mobile phones can also increase poverty due to consumptive forms of appropriation and practices such as those touched upon in Chapter 2. In Kenya, a study published in 2008 found that the poorest 75% of the population using mobile phones spent 22% of their income on them; and in 2010 the cost of a minute long call off- network in Niger, $0.38 per minute, amounted to 40% of a household's daily income.[152] In Tanzania, research among university students in 2009 found that they were spending five times more on mobile phone connectivity than on food, which raises concerns regarding development added-value, considering that youth are drawn to social media platforms, talking on the phone all night ('MTN Cool') or accessing music, movies and pornographic websites (Nyakokombo).[153] The price of telecommunications has considerably decreased since these studies were published. Still, villagers in Nyakokombo spent around 12% of their yearly income on mobile phones, and mobile telephony-related spending in sub-Saharan Africa still ranks fourth behind food, housing and health. In 2014, 17 out of the top 20 developing nations with the highest monthly percentage of subscriber income spent on operating a mobile phone were found south of the Sahara.[154] Even if mobile phones are not used for business, their perceived conduciveness for long-term prosperity is sufficient to make Africans sacrifice basic needs for them. While mobile phones provide social and economic utility, often times such utility and the willingness of subscribers to incur high costs is a matter of social status and reflects fears of exclusion from the process of globalization (Carmody 2012: 8). Too often the phone has become an index of development rather than a driver of development, a social marker rather than a source of income.

Along with important financial costs, the use of mobile phones can cause significant social strains which are often not considered in the ICT4D paradigm.

The fact that mobile phones are digitally bridging the 'rural-urban' divide inasmuch as they permit instantaneous communication between villagers and urbanites is a social revolution not welcomed by all. The compression of time and space by technologies like mobile telephony increases the speed of life and with it the gap between *actual* and *potential* acceleration, as well as 'between what technologies *can* do and what they *do* do' (Larkin 2008). Mobile phones, like roads and railways, operate also on the level of fantasy and desire as they symbolize the 'promises of a better world' (Archambault 2017: 2). Space-time compression, however, often generates both fascination and terror, and can also enhance a sense of restlessness and dissatisfaction with one's current station in life. As Jacques Ellul argues in his classic *The Technological Society*, technologies can 'suppress the respite of time indispensable to the rhythm of life' (Ellul 1964: 329). While mobile telephony compresses distance, it also brings distance home to people. Mobile phones not only facilitate the physical migration process but also play a role in motivating more West Africans to migrate to supposedly greener pastures within their countries (rural-urban exodus), the wider sub-Saharan region, Europe and other parts of the world (De Bruijn 2009: 16).

As is well documented, African migration to Europe has also increased in recent years. In 2016, Frontex, the European Agency for border control, estimated that 93% of migrants arriving in Italy came from Africa. Most originated from West Africa with Nigeria, Guinea and Ivory Coast alone accounting for a third of the arrivals. Nine out of the top ten nationalities reaching Italian shores in 2016 were African, and ten times more African migrants made the journey in 2016 than in 2010.[155] Similarly, in the United States the number of migrants from sub-Saharan Africa has doubled every ten years since the 1970s. It reached a peak between 2000 and 2010 when more sub-Saharan Africans arrived than during the three-hundred years of the transatlantic slave trade.[156] Mobile phones have surely not been the sole factor causing this surge in migration since the turn of the century. Nonetheless, by the information they relay – such as through Facebook, which is often used as a travel agency platform to lure West African migrants – they undeniably shape the imaginary of Africans as well as they facilitate the migration process.[157] Mobile phones have become indispensable tools to stay in touch with, and be 'remote-controlled' by, human traffickers on the long journey to Europe. They have also become life-saving devices for migrants crossing the Mediterranean Sea – and sometimes life-risking devices as they lure migrants into accepting ever lower standards of seaworthiness and trusting that their emergency call will permit humanitarian rescuers to arrive in good time to save them in case of shipwreck (Smith 2018: 174-177). Due to mobile phones, African immigrants, as well as 'bushfallers', also increasingly feel the weight of negotiating remittances that can now be transferred by mobile money.

The ease of communication comes with heightened demand as rural dwellers can now easily reach their urban kin as well as with family members abroad. Under the realm of ubuntuism, this has raised new questions of collective identity and individual agency, and heightened the tension between liberty and obligations and collective success versus excuses for opportunism. Mobile phones have extended the long arm of the home village to remind migrants of their responsibilities, and while communication is the reward, the inclusivity that it necessitates is the price (Nyamnjoh et al. 2016: 107-108). In 2015, mobile phones and mobile money facilitated the transfer of $35.2 billion from African migrants to their country of origin.[158] Africans living abroad would be able to remit even more if it wasn't for a remittance 'supertax' of nearly $2 billion per year, which amounts to an average transfer cost of 12%

compared to the global average of 7.2% (Nyamnjoh et al. 2016: 11). Western Union and MoneyGram control two-thirds of the African market and take advantage of weak competition concentration of market power and financial regulation to charge high prices for remitting to Africa. Such efforts to send money back home have surely led to beneficial initiatives but have also exacerbated a culture of dependency on privatized aid in sub-Saharan Africa, which per capita has been the most assisted region in the world for the past sixty years while also remaining the most underdeveloped.

The detrimental effects of mobile phone use are not unique to West Africa and have been well-documented in other regions of the world. Mobile phones have been banned in schools from New York City to the district of Nyakokombo. Recognizing their drawbacks undermines the hope that mobile telephony might be a panacea for development in sub-Saharan Africa. In 2013, more than a decade after the arrival of mobile phones, the ten countries with the highest proportion of citizens living in extreme poverty – less than $1.25 per day – were all still found in sub-Saharan Africa.[159] In 2017, two citizens out of three south of the Sahara did not have access to electricity, and approximately 300 million did not have access to clean water.[160] The consumption of electricity in all of sub-Saharan Africa – 48 countries, about 1 billion people – is lower than that of Spain with less than 50 million inhabitants.[161] At the very least, mobile telephony is not a quick-fix for deeply entrenched underdevelopment. In this regard, the ICT4D paradigm seems fundamentally flawed in that it assumes a linear progression that all countries must follow and ascribes mobile phones the potential to allow 'backward' nations to 'catch-up'. But the United States or Europe have never been where sub-Saharan Africa positions itself currently – with mud huts and smartphones co-existing. While underdeveloped by any measure, sub-Saharan Africa is not lagging behind but, rather, on a different plane or elsewhere.

## C. African Modernity

In 1867, Karl Marx stated in *Das Kapital* that 'the industrially more developed country presents to the less developed country a picture of the latter's future' (Marx 1867). Nearly a century later, in 1951, economic historian Alexander Gerschenkron published *Economic Backwardness in Historical Perspective*, in which he nuances Marx's analysis by arguing that 'by the very virtue of its backwardness' the development of a low-income nation may differ fundamentally from that of an advanced country (Gerschenkron 1951: 7). Nonetheless, Gerschenkron's argument and work also rests on the notion that there are linear stages of economic development and that the process goes forward in largely determined stages. In 1959, economist W.W. Rostow identified these phases of development as the following: 1.) traditional society; 2.) preconditions for take-off; 3.) take-off; 4.) drive to maturity; and 5.) an age of high mass consumption.[162] Since Rostow's time the linear-stage model of development has been heavily criticized but is still widely prevalent in the field of economics – most notably championed by Jeffrey Sachs and his 'Big Push' theory (Sachs 2005). The ICT4D paradigm is largely analogous with, and influenced by, the ascendant stage theory as it praises the potential of mobile phones to help leapfrog 'stages' of development and bring 'modernity' to sub-Saharan Africa for it to 'catch-up' with wealthier regions of the world. Yet, if one were to apply Rostow's analytic grid to contemporary West Africa, one would have to conclude that the region is in all of his five 'stages' at once.

Frederick Cooper, a noted historian of Africa, cautions against such 'backward readings' of history as a race or 'tale of progress… privileging "the West" and evaluating the history of every other place in terms of "lacks"' (Cooper 2000: 318). Cooper argues that historical analysis should inform us about how the world came to be a place where certain countries have a GNP per capita one hundred times that of others and where the eight richest people possess as much wealth as the bottom half of the world population. While concepts and umbrella terms such as 'progress' or 'development' are much criticized, 'the distinctions that such words point to are very concrete part of people's lives' (Cooper 2000: 319). As such, while history does not offer lessons, 'it does suggest possibilities' (Cooper 2000: 312). Cooper rejects a 'history that confines the zigzags of time into linear pathways' and which privileges states over all other forms of human connection to tell a story of 'development', invariably leaving Africans on the margins (Cooper 2000: 298). Such interpretations of progress infer that populations south of the Sahara are lacking some 'crucial characteristic necessary to attain what is otherwise "universal"' (Ibid). Viewed in this light, the rapid adoption of mobile phones has generated hope for the advent of modernity in sub-Saharan Africa. While this is not the fact in the straight-forward way that underlies such expectations, it still holds true that cellphones south of the Sahara are part of a 'newness' which, in its unique conjunction with the 'old', makes sub-Saharan Africa a very modern place. The rise of mobile phones has encouraged entrepreneurs in other sectors to turn obstacles to 'development' into opportunities for African modernity. For example, building on their success in East Africa, off-grid-solar power startups are pouring into West Africa, offering solar kits and pay-as-you-go solar home systems (SHSs) to the millions who lack reliable access to electricity. SHSs customers pay a small up front amount for the equipment and then monthly or weekly payments for the energy used through mobile money. This formula enabled by mobile phones allows customers to pay for the level of energy based on their needs and budget, which also reduces risks of nonpayment for suppliers. With small-scale solar power expansion, phone charging costs – like kerosene, batteries, candles or diesel for generators – have decreased and the sub-Saharan region has the opportunity to leapfrog the power grid 'stage of development'. By 2030, 80% of the global off-grid population is predicted to be south of the Sahara – solar power having become the main source of energy.[163] Here, 4G networks coexist with 'talking drums', mobile phones are charged on top of huts using solar panels, and tradi-practitioners use mobile phones for distance healing.

Voices simultaneously rise to criticize the march of progress within the capitalist system – on the basis that the rich get richer at the expense of the poor – as much as they are prone to laud the penetration of mobile telephony in Africa and quick to associate it with development. But, what added value for development is accrued by watching pornography on mobile phones? Or in facilitating 'scamming' and thefts? Sometimes mobile phones bring progress, but at other times it is much less evident, especially considering the costs of mobile telephony. Either way, positing mobile phones as a technical fix for deeper-rooted economic and social challenges in sub-Saharan Africa takes the focus away from how these disparities are produced, which is important if they are to be overcome. Likewise, the hope that mobile phones will help leapfrog development stages overlooks the drawbacks of leapfrogging. When the rate of technological advancement greatly outstrips that of economic growth, fractures occur, as shown in the case of ActivSpaces in Buea and the lack of widespread adoption of mobile applications by the Cameroonian population. Rather than helping those who need it most, like the midwife in Nyakokombo, most mobile applications like 'GiftedMom' are only available on Androids and as such primarily accessible for the wealthier and oftentimes better educated segment of the population. This is also the case in other parts of sub-Saharan Africa, such as South Africa where, in 2015, 57% of the population with a secondary education owned a smartphone versus 13% with less education.[164] Unequal access to smartphones and mobile applications has raised concerns about the rise of a new 'digital divide' and the enhancement of already stark inequalities.

Attention also needs to be paid to the unprecedented demographic growth and, as a consequence, exceptionally youthful population age structure south of the Sahara. For instance, today in Lagos, a mega-city of well over 20 million and the economic center of West Africa, 60% of the population is less than fifteen years old – against 14% in Paris (Smith 2018: 59). A 'young Lagosian' is almost a redundant statement. And all over sub-Saharan Africa, the youth – 'small' people in traditional parlance – represent the vast majority of the population. With the spread of 4G technology, which permits easy access to the internet, these young Africans – the 'Android generation' – become the vessels of globalization. 'Connected' to the outside world like never before, they put a premium on anything 'global' and thus enhance what the French political scientist Jean-François Bayart calls Africa's 'historic extraversion' – a sort of 'cargo cult' ascribing extra value to what comes from abroad and, at least implicitly, depreciating the 'local'. This tips the balance of 'glocalization' in hazardous ways. It also creates the conditions for an intergenerational 'stress test' as the young increasingly challenge the 'principle of seniority' which, traditionally but less and less so in the developed world, confers prestige, wealth and power to elders, in fact old men. As a consequence, in the years to come, mobile telephony is likely to play the role of a catalyst for fundamental change – the demise of gerontocracy – in sub-Saharan Africa.

Like the youthful demographics south of the Sahara, the rapid dissemination and 'glocalization' of mobile phones is both 'positive' and 'negative'. Yet, as evidenced by several ethnographically informed studies, the link between ICTs and development rests more on 'wishful thinking than on empirical findings' (Archambault 2017: 6). Likewise, this research cautions against ungrounded optimism inasmuch as it demonstrates that mobile phones are *necessary* but not *sufficient* conditions for development. Mobile telephony is no exception to the dependence on outside or foreign 'know-how' which is pervasive in sub-Saharan Africa, a region where mobile phones have yet to be produced on a large scale. This raises concerns linked to the neutrality of the technology and the tension at play between 'globalizers' and 'globalized'.

## Notes

143 172 of the 420 million unique subscribers are in West Africa. Manuel Castells. *End of millennium.* Malden (MA: Blackwell Publishers, 1998), 166-170.

144 GSMA. *The Mobile Economy – sub-Saharan Africa, 2017,* 3.

145 Kevin Donovan and Aaron Martin, 'The Rise of African SIM Registration: The Emerging Dynamics of Regulatory Change' (*First Monday,* 3 Feb. 2014.)

146 GSMA. *The Mobile Economy – sub-Saharan Africa, 2017,* 2.

147 'World Population Prospects'. *United Nations,* 2015, 4.

148 GSMA. *The Mobile Economy – sub-Saharan Africa, 2017,* 3.

149 Jonathan Donner, 'Research Approaches to Mobile Use in the Developing World: A Review of the Literature' (Information Society 24, 2008), 140-59.

150 'World Development Report 2016: Digital Dividends'. *World Bank,* 17 May 2016.

151 Alison Gillwald and Christophe Stork, 'Towards evidence- based ICT policy and regulation: ICT access and usage in Africa', *ResearchICTAFrica.net,* 2008.

152 Gillwald and Stork, 'Towards evidence based ICT policy'; Jenny C. Aker and Isaac Mbiti, 'Mobile phones and economic development', 227.

153 Dorothea Kleine and Tim Unwin, Technological revolution, evolution and new dependencies: What's new about ICT4D? *Third World Quarterly, vol. 30 no. 5* (2009).

154 Tariq Khokhar, 'Where Are the Cheapest and Most Expensive Countries to Own a Mobile Phone?' *The Data Blog,* 20 Jan. 2016.

155 Arnaud Leparmentier and Maryline Baumard. 'Migrations Africaines, le défi de demain'. (*Le Monde.fr*, 16 Jan. 2017.)

156 Sam Roberts, 'Influx of African Immigrants Shifting National and New York Demographics'. *The New York Times*, The New York Times, 1 Sept. 2014.

157 Chantal Da Silva, 'Facebook Must Do More to Crack down on People Smugglers Luring Migrants on Site, UN Migration Agency Says'. *The Independent*, Independent Digital News and Media, 11 Dec. 2017.

158 'Africa's Diaspora Remittances Rise to $35.2 Bn in 2015 - World Bank'. *Africanews*, Africanews, 20 Apr. 2016.

159 Gallup, Inc., 'More Than One in Five Worldwide Living in Extreme Poverty'. *Gallup.com*, 23 Dec. 2013.

160 'La difficile équation de l'eau potable en Afrique'. *Africanews*, Africanews, 23 Mar. 2016.

161 'Énergie, population et planète: Rapport 2015 sur les progrès en Afrique', *Africa Progress Panel*, 12.

162 Walt Whitman Rostow, 'The Stages of Economic Growth'. *The Economic History Review*, vol. 12, no. 1, (1959), pp. 1–16. *JSTOR*.

163 Bavier, Joe. 'Off-Grid Power Pioneers Pour into West Africa'. *Reuters*, Thomson Reuters, 20 Feb. 2018

164 'Cell Phones in Africa: Communication Lifeline'. *Pew Research Center's Global Attitudes Project*, 15 Apr. 2015, 2.

# Conclusion

## A. 'Globalizers' and 'Globalized'

I arrived in Conakry with the preconceived idea that MTN should acculturate their operations better than Orange by virtue of being an African brand. I soon found out that MTN were the ones who made the mistake of focusing their investments on the capital-city Conakry, not recognizing the importance of rural kin for urban dwellers. Their investment on Wi-Max technology also proved to be a mistake. Orange arrived after MTN and rapidly adapted their offers to local needs and realities to increase their market share. I was also curious to find out whether Guineans subscribe to MTN at least partly to support a successful African multinational company. Once again, I was wrong. Many don't even know that MTN is South African and the rest don't seem to care. After all, investments by foreign companies and the privatization of the telecommunications sector, led to the spread of mobile telephony in Africa. Many subscribers mentioned loyalty towards MTN as part of their decision-making, but they are loyal because MTN was the first to make SIMs and communication services affordable, not because it is African. In vain, I continued to ask dog-whistle questions looking for someone to offer reasons why an African brand would acculturate mobile telephony to the needs of their 'fellow Africans' better than a French brand – despite the fact that Orange's staff is also exclusively African and that I actually don't know what 'African' means beyond geography or, as James Ferguson calls it, 'a place-in-the-world' (Ferguson 2006: 4). I was politely reminded that MTN's main shareholders are South African, and that I was in Guinea. At best, some acknowledged that it was encouraging to see an African brand doing well internationally. But the vast majority asserted that they subscribed to mobile operators based on their network and quality of service. MTN, amongst other things, uses Foot Soldiers; introduced Axon; sponsors education with Y'ello care; and offers culturally relevant bonus bundles. Yet, what truly matters to subscribers is network coverage. Subscribers purchase credit and want their calls to go through, which has little to do with acculturation. The company that can best provide these services, i.e. for the time being Orange, has a larger share of the market. According to this line of thought, as long as mobile phones work properly it does not matter that they are produced in China. Nor is it of particular significance that Westerners invented mobile phones. If 'ownership' in this deeper sense is irrelevant to West Africans, then we should assume that mobile telephony is neutral. But, in light of my findings, the 'neutrality hypothesis' is only one side of the story.

The tension between 'globalizers' and 'globalized' lies at the heart of this research. What does it change to be the user rather than the inventor of mobile telephony? Are those who possess the technology necessarily the 'globalizers'? Mobile phones were invented by non-Africans. If technology is not neutral, then are Africans being 'alienated'? According to Appiah, as mentioned in Chapter 1, 'machines are now as African as novelists' (Appiah 1991: 357). The difference for Africans, however, is that novels are the fruit of their thoughts and labor, they are 'theirs'; mobile phones are the product of inventors and technicians outside of Africa and thus, by definition, 'foreign' or 'other'. Appiah's interpretation of the *Yoruba Man with a Bicycle,* appears at first glance simplistic, if not naïve. Yet, by virtue of being from the West, am I more likely to use a mobile phone or a bicycle better than an African would? I don't think so. Piot, in *Remotely Global,* supports Appiah's argument in that he interprets the adoption of Western goods by Africans not as a form of capitulation but rather as a process of appropriation by which foreign goods retain aspects of their alterity but are refigured in locally meaningful ways. They retain 'alterity' but are altered in turn and become hybrid – 'glocalized' – objects.[164] Nonetheless, in my opinion, not being the inventor or producer of such objects is a form of capitulation, or at the very least a sign of power-differential. Those who invent are more powerful, they hoard the 'strategic agency' that reshapes the world; those who merely use new inventions dispose only of 'tactical agency' as they adapt to the changes in their lives brought about by others, in a West African perspective: from 'outside'. Moreover, the forms of 'resistance' exercised by Africans in the process of appropriation also come at a price. While the call-box and SIM registration systems are tailored to the local setting, they are also often jarringly disorganized and inefficient. Giving money to the bread deliverer to be dropped off at the Orange agency in town, is neither an effective nor a sustainable way for call-boxers in Nyakokombo to receive credit. Local agency often makes up for infrastructural or corporate shortcomings, while also hiding the need for better organization. While discovering the different ways to charge phones in Nyakokombo, the mobile call-boxers in Yaoundé, or the young entrepreneurs developing apps in Buea, Naipaul's 'people are the most creative when things are very perturbed' kept ringing in my ear (French 2008: 273).

Consonant with its argument about 'glocalization', this research interprets modernity as a global concept which is refracted locally in different ways and, as such, certainly not synonymous with 'Westernization'. The planet-spanning homogenizing narrative is just that, a narrative – neglectful of the relevance of the local. This research highlights creative forms of appropriation by West African users of mobile telephony. Yet, it would betray its findings if, in turn, it were to neglect the 'field' defined by mobile operators, and the boundaries that are intrinsic to mobile telephony. The villager in Babanki ambling around with his mobile landline-type phone made in Japan is the exception to the rule. While media outlets and the ICT4D narrative often focus on the new mobile applications susceptible to 'revolutionize' the continent and the creative uses of mobile phones in Africa, the tree should not hide the forest. It is misguided to speak of an 'African' way of using mobile phones or an 'African' modernity as a result of cellular appropriation and acculturation.

African modernity is modernity in Africa, distinct only due to differing conditions of emergence. However, there is no compelling reason to call into question the global concept of modernity, as there is no reason to let go of the universal idea of, let's say, a table simply because there are high tables in the dining halls of British colleges and short-legged tables in *minkas*, the traditional Japanese houses. By the same token, as much as mobile phones in West Africa are reshaped in the processes of appropriation and acculturation, the universal idea of 'a mobile phone' remains. Mobile phones south of the Sahara have been appropriated in ways unforeseen by their creators, but they have not been 'reinvented' and are still primarily used for their basic properties: calling and sending messages. For the moment, Africans only have tactical agency. They play a role, but they neither set the scene nor do they write the script. While they can put their cultural sticker on a technology invented and produced by outsiders, Africans are being 'globalized' by mobile telephony more than they globalize their part of the world by using a universal communications technology.

## B. Limitations and Future Research

We should be cautious not to look for arguments to ratify historical outcomes in hindsight. When mobile phones were first created, no one predicted that Africa would be among the dynamic markets for mobile telephony in the ensuing decade. In hindsight, arguments are made to explain this phenomenon, creating a sense of causality when in reality it can also be a product of the constraints of narration and the need for coherence. For example, a common explanation for the social adoption of mobile phones in West Africa, touched upon in this book, is that mobile telephony builds on a culture of orality.

While oral traditions of storytelling are still prominent and literacy rates in most West African nations are some of the lowest in the World, European nations adopted mobile telephony despite different backgrounds. Most Guineans, as of now, do not leave a voicemail, because they dismiss the idea of speaking to a machine, but do they prefer calling as a result of cultural habits or because of better offers made by operators? Between 2015 and 2016, in Guinea the total traffic of SMS fell from 5,400 million to 3,100 million as the tax on emitted SMS increased.[165] Likewise, as smartphones are becoming cheaper and more common throughout West Africa, money spent by subscribers on internet data is increasing and encroaching on voice communications. In 2016 alone, the number of Internet mobile subscribers in Guinea grew by 13%.[166] Rapid changes are taking place and what is reality today may not be tomorrow, which also points to the fact that the different forms of appropriation and acculturation put forward in my own research can rapidly become history. Apart for not accounting for these rapid changes, the great weakness of all narratives is that a story well-told 'makes the linkages of narration appear as causally necessary' (Cooper 2000: 309). By exerting violence on the material to 'make it fit', this research lends order to what might be more random if not chaotic. It insinuates an underlying logic – some 'cause' at work – which may only be the result of narration. In doing so, like other narratives, this book constrains the extent to which agency and often times 'luck' combine to shape the adoption of mobile telephony.

Just as this work was driven by the desire to portray Africans in a light other than passive victims of globalization, in my future research I wish to challenge the engrained dichotomy of the rural-urban divide south of the Sahara. In sub-Saharan Africa, village and city seem farther apart than anywhere else in the world, and the rural-urban divide is entrenched in a series of dichotomies: tradition-modernity, immobility-mobility, seniority-youth, stasis-development, gerontocracy-democracy.

However, despite the unequal distribution of smartphones, mobile phones have spread among rural as well as urban dwellers. More than an 'infrastructural turn' or a technological 'leapfrog', the advent of mobile telephony amounts to a social revolution. Now that the village and the city are in constant conversation, the question is not whether the rural-urban divide is affected, but how. I plan to assess the content and the effects of instantaneous communication, which not only bear upon the social structure and collective imaginary but may also ultimately lead to the acceleration or deceleration of the rural exodus. To that end, I have been granted a Research Fulbright to address the transformative change brought by the spread of mobile telephony through a case study in Togo, West Africa. Its capital, Lomé, is part of the urban sprawl along the Atlantic coast between Accra (Ghana) and Lagos (Nigeria) that is expected to coalesce into a vast conurbation within the next twenty years. While much has been written about the unprecedented surge of the African mobile telephony market, scant research has been conducted using mobile telephony as a metric on ways in which this new conversation impacts the rural-urban divide.

Now that urbanites and their rural kin can communicate at any moment, what preponderates in their conversations – notice of sickness or death, of aid requests, of upcoming ceremonies, of commercial opportunities? Are things 'revealed' that used to remain unspoken before in face-to-face meetings? Why do urbanites still engage with an environment they have left? Do the more frequent exchanges bridge or throw into relief the rural-urban divide? Overall, how has the new connectivity affected social relations, norms and values, as well as the Janus-faced rural exodus-urban drift as a whole? In broader terms, my research will explore the emergence of a 'digital lifestyle' or 'mobile phone culture' that villagers and urban dwellers are now sharing, not only through the common usage of mobile telephony but also through their exchange of lived daily experience. I hypothesize that my findings could point to the emergence of a hybrid rural-urban identity in the West African coastal corridor and an acceleration or reversal of the rural-exodus. Potentially, this study will also offer a template for subsequent research in other parts of the developing world to put my claim to the test. For example, in regions of South America or Asia where mobile telephony spread earlier than south of the Sahara, its impact on rural-urban migration already might be measurable by now.

## Notes

164 The award winning documentary *Makala*, released in 2017, quite literally illustrates Appiah's argument. It follows a young man in Congo, named Kabwita, on the trek from his village to the city to sell charcoal. Kabwita ties the charcoal on the bicycle with ropes and for 30 miles he uses two wooden sticks attached on the bicycle to maintain control and push it forward – in doing so, Kabwita tailors the bicycle to his needs inasmuch as it becomes 'Other'.

165 ARPT Rapport Annuel, 2016

166 ARPT Rapport 3ème trimestre, 5-6

# Bibliography

## Primary Sources

Abdelkrim, Samir. 'Au Cameroun, comment une start-up lutte contre les cancers féminins.' *Le Monde.fr*, Le Monde, 7 June 2018.

Adogla-Bessa, Delali. 'Nana Addo Launches Ghana's Digital Property Address System.' *Citifmonline.com*, 18 Oct. 2017.

'Africa's Diaspora Remittances Rise to $35.2 Bn in 2015 - World Bank.' *Africanews*, Africanews, 20 Apr. 2016.

'Africa Internet Users, 2017 Population and Facebook Statistics.' *Internet World Stats*.

'Afrique: ces applications agricoles qui boostent le Ghana.' *Le Point Afrique*, 9 Jan. 2018.

'Annuaire Statistique du Cameroun, édition 2015', Institut National de la Statistique.

Bensimon, Cyril. 'Au Cameroun, pour continuer de rayonner, Douala contrainte de se réinventer.' *Le Monde.fr*, Le Monde, 23 Aug. 2017.

'Buea, La Silicon Valley Du Cameroun - BBC Afrique.' *BBC News*, BBC.

'Cameroon by IT Statistics.' *Gamo Nana*, 7 May 2016.

'Cameroun: Le gouvernement va en guerre contre la propagation des fausses nouvelles sur internet.' *TIC Mag*, 16 Jan. 2017.

'Cameroon's Mobile Penetration Hits 80%.' *Telecompaper*, 12 Feb. 2016.

'Cameroon: Orange and MTN Monopolise 93.8% of the Telephone Market.' *Business in Cameroon*, 7 Feb. 2016.

'Cameroon to Increase Minimum Wage from De 28,000 to 36,270 FCFA.' *Business in Cameroon*, 22 July 2014.

*Cameroon: Poverty Reduction Strategy Paper.* The International Monetary Fund, 2010.

CamTel Bamenda Service Head for Technical Matters, Interview 17/10/16

'Cell Phones in Africa: Communication Lifeline.' *Pew Research Center's Global Attitudes Project*, 15 Apr. 2015.

CIA World Factbook, 2016.

'Churchill and the Commons Chamber.' *UK Parliament*, Oct. 1943.

Countrymeters.info. 'Cameroon Population.' *Countrymeters*.

Daily Mail: 'Pregnant woman left to die on steps of Cameroon hospital because she had no money to pay for treatment as relatives tried to in vain to deliver twins alive,' 03/14/16.

Dell'amore, Christine. 'The Humans of the Bird World.' *National Geographic*, National Geographic Society, June 2018

Diallo, Oumar. 'Guinée: MTN lance son programme d'assistance sociale "Y'ello Care' actualité de la Guinée.' *Aminata*, Aminata.com les nouvelles de la république de Guinée, 10 June 2017.

Emery, David. 'Beware of Calls from These 'Killer Phone Numbers."' *Thought Co*, 9 Apr. 2018.

'Énergie, population et planète: Rapport 2015 sur les progrès en Afrique', *Africa Progress Panel*, 12.

Fernholz, Tim. 'More People around the World Have Cell Phones than Ever Had Land-Lines.' *Quartz*, Quartz, 25 Feb. 2014.

'Fixed Telephone Subscriptions (per 100 People).' *World Bank Data*.

'GhanaPostGPS.' *Ghana Post GPS*.

'Global Findex Data: Sub-Saharan Africa.' *The World Bank*, 2014.

Goodwin, Richard. 'The History of Mobile Phones From 1973 To 2008: The Handsets That Made It ALL Happen.' *Know Your Mobile*, Know Your Mobile, 6 Mar. 2017.

GSMA. *The Mobile Economy – sub-Saharan Africa, 2017,* pp. 1-52.

'Human Development Reports.' | *Human Development Reports*.

'ICTs Delivering Home-Grown Development Solutions in Africa.' *World Bank*, 2012.

'In Much of Sub-Saharan Africa, Mobile Phones Are More Common than Access to Electricity.' *The Economist*, Newspaper, 8 Nov. 2017.

Khokhar, Tariq. 'Where Are the Cheapest and Most Expensive Countries to Own a Mobile Phone?' *The Data Blog*, 20 Jan. 2016.

Linning, Stephanie. 'Pregnant Woman Left to Die on Steps of Cameroon Hospital Because She Had No Money to Pay for Treatment as Relatives Tried to in Vain to Deliver Twins Alive.' *Daily Mail Online*, Associated Newspapers, 14 Mar. 2016.

'L'interdiction des téléphones portables à l'école fait aussi débat à l'étranger.' *Le Monde.fr*, Le Monde, 14 Dec. 2017.

M&G Africa. 'There Are Always Surprises: 11 Bank-Breaking Facts about Mobile Money and Africa.' *MG Africa*, 29 Feb. 2016.

'Memory Cards 20 Products Found.' *Memory Cards - Buy Online | Jumia Cameroun*.

'Missions.' *Telecommunications Regulatory Board*.

'Mobile App Breaks Sex Taboos In Cameroon - Page 2 of 3.' *Working Woman Report*, 2 Oct. 2016.

'Mobile Cellular Subscriptions.' *World Bank Data*.

'Mobile Money Ready for Take-off in Cameroon.' *Business in Cameroon*, No. 28, 3 June 2015, pp. 1–34.

Moh, Catharina. 'How a Speedy Emergency Services App Is Saving Lives.' *BBC News*, BBC, 24 Nov. 2017.

Monks, Kieron. 'Cameroon Goes Offline after Anglophone Revolt.' *CNN*, Cable News Network, 2 Jan. 2018.

Monks, Kieron. 'M-Pesa: Kenya's Mobile Success Story Turns 10.' *CNN*, Cable News Network, 24 Feb. 2017.

'Most Popular Messaging Apps 2017.' *Statista*.

'MTN about Us, Who We Are.' *MTN*.

Nicol, Jake et al. 'Inside the Vast (and Growing) Global Trade in Stolen Smart Phones.' *National Geographic*, National Geographic Society, 9 Sept. 2015.

139

Parke, Phoebe. 'How Many People Use Social Media in Africa?' *CNN*, Cable News Network, 14 Jan. 2016.

'The Company That Ruled the Waves.' *The Economist*, Newspaper, 17 Dec. 2011.

'The General Conference of the International Labour Organization.' *International Labour Organization*, 2002.

'The Indian Ocean Trade: A Classroom Simulation" African Studies Center | Boston University.' *African Studies Center RSS*

'The Mobile Economy, West Africa 2017.' *GSMA* report.

RFI. 'Vers un réseau téléphonique unique en Afrique - RFI.' *RFI Afrique*, Rfi, 30 Mar. 2018.

Richter, Felix. 'Infographic: Mobile Subscriptions to Outnumber the World's Population.' *Statista Infographics*, 17 Nov. 2015.

Seward, Zachary M. 'The First Mobile Phone Call Was Made 40 Years Ago Today.' *The Atlantic*, Atlantic Media Company, 3 Apr. 2013.

Schmitt, Eric and Rukmini Callimachi. 'Niger Ambush Suspect May Be in Custody, Officials Say.' *The New York Times*, 16 Apr. 2018.

Singh Mankotia, Anandita. 'Make Biometric Proof Must to Buy Sim Card: Delhi Police Commissioner | Gadgets Now.' *Gadget Now*, 21 June 2013

SIT class with traditional doctors, 10/24/16: 'you must believe to heal, if you don't believe you will not heal'

Sophie Eastaugh. 'Solar-Cart Can Charge 80 Cell Phones at Once.' *CNN*, Cable News Network, 24 Oct. 2017.

Spector, Dina. 'What Is WiMax? And How Does It Work?' *Business Insider*, Business Insider, 23 Sept. 2010.

'Sport fin du tournoi SMUS sponsorisé par MTN Guinée...' *Africaguinee.com - Site Officiel d'informations sur la Guinée et l'Afrique*, 3 May 2017.

Sub Saharan Africa Mobile Cellular Subscriptions Per 100 People.' *Trading Economics*.

'Suspended since Two Weeks, Vodafone Cameroon Submit a Request for License.' *Business in Cameroon*, 26 Sept. 2017.

Veselinovic, Milena. 'This 23-Year-Old Is Saving Mothers with an App.' *CNN*, Cable News Network, 17 Feb. 2015.

'Viettel: Vietnamese Shareholders Not Above the Law.' *CamerounWeb*, 7 Oct. 2014,

'Welcome to Orange Cameroon.' *About Orange Cameroon | Orange Cameroun*,

'Welcome to 'Silicon Mountain,' Africa's next Tech Hub.' *The France 24 Observers*, France 24, 23 Sept. 2016.

'World Development Report 2016: Digital Dividends.' *World Bank*, 17 May 2016.

'Y'ello Care.' *MTN Group*.

## Interviews

*Cameroon*

Observation made during pilot-research in Bamenda, 10/16/16

SIT class with traditional doctors, 10/24/16

Interview with Professor Blaise Nande at the University of Buea, 11/15/16

Interview with call-boxer in Yaoundé 11/09/16

Interview with Chawa in Buea, Student at the University of Buea, 11/16/16

Interview with Fritz Ekwoge at the Annual gathering of ActivSpaces in Buea, Founder of *Feem*, 11/16/16

Interview with Ngae Denis in Yaoundé, The Director of Infrastructures and Networks access at the MINPOSTEL Interview, 11/10/16

Interview with Professor Akama at the University of Buea, 11/16/16

Interview with Valéry Colong at the Annual Gathering of ActivSpaces in Buea, Co-Founder of ActivSpaces, 11/16/16

Interview with Dr. Soney in Buea, Director of the College of Technology at the University of Buea, 11/17/16

Interview in Buea with Christian, Assistant Lecturer at the College of Technology at the University of Buea, 11/17/16

Interview with Mathieu Youbi in Yaoundé, Founder of LCCLC, in Yaoundé, 11/24/16

Interview with Professor Walter Gam Nkwi at the University of Buea, 11/18/16

Interview with Kingsley in Buea, 11/17/16

Interview with Proxy on Avenue Kennedy, phone salesman, 11/25/16

Interview with Professor Njoya at the University of Yaoundé, 11/30/16

Interview with teacher in Nyakokombo, 11/12/16

Interview with cocoa farmer in Nyakokombo, 11/11/16

Questionnaire Chief of Orange Agency in Bamenda, 11/10/16

*Guinea*

Interview and field research with Ibrahima Ba in Ratoma, Conakry, Sales coordinator at MTN-Guinea, 06/10/17

Interview with Mariama Djéllo Diallo in Conakry, Head of Customer Relations at MTN-Guinea, 06/10/17

Observation at Customer Relations, Headquarters of MTN-Guinea in Conakry, 06/10/17

Interview with Lalla Cheriff in Conakry, Manager of Brand and Communication at MTN-Guinea, 06/10/17

Interview with Amadou Diallo in Conakry, Agent of Data and Devices Management at MTN-Guinea, 06/11/17

Interview and field research with Lawrence Ngalah in Kindia, Head of Sales and Distribution at MTN-Guinea, 06/14/17

Interview with Reuben Opata in Conakry, Director of Information Technology at MTN-Guinea, 06/18/17

Interview with Papa Sow in Conakry, CEO of MTN-Guinea, 06/20/17

## Secondary Sources

Abu-Lughod, Janet L. *Before European Hegemony: the World System A.D. 1250-1350.* Oxford University Press, 2006.

Aglionby, John. 'Financial Times Fintech Takes off in Africa as Lenders Tap Mobile Technology.' *Financial Times,* 16 May 2016.

Alexander, Alex, Lin Shi, and Bensam Solomon. 'How Fintech Is Reaching the Poor in Africa and Asia: a Start-up Perspective.' *World Bank Group,* Mar. 2017.

Aker, Jenny C. and Isaac M. Mbiti. 'Mobile Phones and Economic Development in Africa.' *Journal of Economic Perspectives,* vol. 24, no. 3, 2010, pp. 207–232.

Aker, Jenny C., Paul Collier, and Pedro C. Vincente. *Is information power? Using cell phones during an election in Mozambique. Mimeo,* 2011.

Appadurai, Arjun. *Disjuncture and Difference in the Global Cultural Economy.* Theory, Culture and Society, 1990.

Appiah, Kwame Anthony. 'Is the Post- in Postmodernism the Post- in Postcolonial?' *Critical Inquiry,* vol. 17, no. 2, 1991, pp. 336–357.

Archambault, Julie Soleil. *Mobile Secrets: Youth, Intimacy, and the Politics of Pretense in Mozambique.* The University of Chicago Press, 2017.

Aristotle, *Poetics.* Translated by Malcom Heath, Penguin Classics, 1997.

Banisar, David. 'Privacy and data protection around the world,' *Proceedings of the 21st International Conference on Privacy and Personal Data Protection,* 1999.

Bar, François et. al., 'Mobile technology appropriation in a distant mirror: Baroque infiltration, Creolization, and Cannibalism.' Paper presented at the Seminário sobre Desarrollo Económico, Desarrollo Social y Comunicaciones Móviles en América Latina, Buenos Aires, 20–21 (April, 2010).

Barber, Benjamin R. *Jihad vs. McWorld*, Times Books, 1995.

Bates, Robert H. *Prosperity and Violence: The Political Economy of Development*. W.W. Norton, 2010.

Bavier, Joe. 'Off-Grid Power Pioneers Pour into West Africa'. *Reuters*, Thomson Reuters, 20 Feb. 2018

Binsbergen, Wim van. 'Can ICT Belong in Africa, or is ICT Owned by the North Atlantic Region?' In Situating Globality: African Agency in the Appropriation of Global Culture. Leiden: Brill, 2004, 107-55.

Blacker, David. 'On the Alleged Neutrality of Technology: A Study in Dewey's Experience and Nature.' *The Journal of Speculative Philosophy*, vol. 8, no. 4, 1994, pp. 297–317.

Bonhomme, Julien. 'The Dangers of Anonymity: Witchcraft, Rumor, and Modernity in Africa.' *HAU: Journal of Ethnographic Theory*, vol. 2, no. 2, 2012, pp. 205–233.

Bourdieu, Pierre. 'The Forms of Capital.' *Handbook of Theory and Research for the Sociology of Education*, edited by John G. Richardson, Greenwood Press, 1986, pp. 241–258.

Bradley J. Raynor. 'Informal Transportation and Associations: A Case Study of the Boda Boda,' Undergraduate Honors Thesis at Kenyon College, 2015.

Brown, Heather. Emily Guskin and Amy Mitchell. 'The Role of Social Media in the Arab Uprisings.' *Pew Research Center's Journalism Project*, 28 Nov. 2012.

Bruijn, Mirjam de and Francis Nyamnjoh. *Mobile Phones: The New Talking Drums of Africa*. Langaa Rpcig, 2009.

Bruijn, Mirjam de. *The Telephone Has Grown Legs'. Mobile Communication and Social Change in the Margins of African Society*. African Studies Centre: Leiden, The Netherlands, 2008.

Butler, Rhette. 'Cell Phones May Help 'Save' Africa.' Mongabay, 2005.

Carmody, Pádraig. 'The Informationalization of Poverty in Africa? Mobile Phones and Economic Structure.' *Information Technologies & International Development*, 2012.

Castelli, Enrico. *Le temps harcelant*. Presses Universitaires de France, 1952.

Castells, Manuel. *End of millennium*. Malden MA: Blackwell Publishers, 1998.

Castells, Manuel. *The Rise of the Network Society*. The Information Age: Economy, Society and Culture. Oxford: Wiley-Blackwell, 2000.

Chandler, Daniel. 'Technology as Neutral or Non-Neutral.' *Technological or Media Determinism*, 2014.

Chéneau-Loquay, Annie. 'Modes d'appropriation innovants du téléphone mobile en Afrique,' Union Internationale des Télécommunications (UIT) Ministère des Affaires Étrangères et Européennes (MAEE), 2010.

Cheru, Fantu. *African Renaissance: Roadmaps to the Challenge of Globalization*. Zed Books Ltd, 2002.

Cooper, Frederick. 'Africa's Pasts and Africa's Historians.' Canadian *Journal of African Studies* vol. 34, no. 2 (2000), 298-336.

Donner, Jonathan. 'Research Approaches to Mobile Use in the Developing World: A Review of the Literature.' Information Society 24, 2008, 140-59.

Donovan, Kevin P., and Aaron K. Martin. 'The Rise of African SIM Registration: The Emerging Dynamics of Regulatory Change.' *First Monday*, 3 Feb. 2014.

Droz, Jean-Pierre, Bernard Carme, Pierre Couppié, Mathieu Nacher and Catherine Thiéblemont, editors. *Tropical Hemato-Oncology*. Springer International Publishing, 2015.

Ekekwe, Ndubuisi. 'How Digital Technology Is Changing Farming in Africa.' *Harvard Business Review*, 18 May 2017.

Ellis, Stephen. 'Tuning in to Pavement Radio.' *African Affairs*, vol. 88, no. 352, 1989, pp. 321–330. *JSTOR*.

Ellul, Jacques. *The Technological Bluff*. Grand Rapids, MI: Eerdmans, 25 Sept. 1990.

Ellul, Jacques. *The Technological Society*. Translated by John Wilkinson, Vintage Books, 1964.

Enyegue. Michel. Doctorate thesis consulted during my study abroad in Cameroon, not available online: «Les raisons du choix d'un opérateur de téléphonie mobile par le consommateur Camerounais», École supérieur des sciences et techniques de l'information et de la communication (ESSTIC), 2002.

Ess, Charles and Fay Sudweeks, editors. *Culture, Technology, Communication: towards an Intercultural Global Village*. State University of New York Press, 2001.

Fanon, Frantz. *Peau noire, masques blancs*. Éditions Du Seuil, 1952.

Ferguson, James. *Global Shadows*. Duke University Press, 2006.

French, Patrick. *The World Is What It Is: The Authorized Biography of V.S. Naipaul*. Picador, 2008.

Friedman, Thomas L. *The Lexus and the Olive Tree*. Random House, 2000.

Friedman, Thomas L. *The World Is Flat: A Brief History of The Twenty-First Century*. Farrar, Straus and Giroux, 2005.

Gillwald, Alison and Christophe Stork. Towards evidence-based ICT policy and regulation: ICT access and usage in Africa, *ResearchICTAfrica.net*, 2008.

Gras, Emmanuel, director. *Makala*. May 2017.

Heeks, Richard. 'i-Development not e-Development: Special issue on ICTs and development.' *Journal of International Development, 14*, (2002).

Hickman, Larry. *John Dewey's Pragmatic Technology*. Indiana University Press, 1990. The Indiana Series in the Philosophy of Technology.

James, Jeffrey. 'Leapfrogging in Mobile Telephony.' *Technological Forecasting & Social Change*, Scribd, 2008.

Johnson, K. 'Mobile or Bust: Cellphones as communication réseau-lution in rural Banyo,' SIT Cameroon Independent Study Project, 2005.

Kleine, Dorothea and Tim Unwin. Technological revolution, evolution and new dependencies: What's new about ICT4D? *Third World Quarterly, vol. 30 no. 5, 2009*.

146

Khondker, Habibul Haque. *Glocalization as Globalization: Evolution of a Sociological Concept.* Bangladesh e-Journal of Sociology, Vol. 1. No. 2, July 2004.

Krings, Matthias. *African Appropriations: Cultural Difference, Mimesis, and Media.* Indiana University Press, 2015.

Larkin, Brian. Signal and Noise: Media, Infrastructure, and Urban Culture in Nigeria. Durham, NC: Duke University Press, 2008.

Lechman, Ewa. *Technological Substitution in Asia.* Routledge, 2017.

Lechner, Frank. 'World Culture Theory.' *The Globalization Website - Theories,* 2001. Accessed October 10th, 2017.

Leparmentier, Arnaud and Maryline Baumard. 'Migrations Africaines, le défi de demain.' *Le Monde.fr,* 16 Jan. 2017.

Mander, Jerry. *Four Arguments for the Elimination of Television.* Harvester Press, 1980.

Marx, Karl. *Das Kapital,* Verlag von Otto Meisne, 1867.

Mendis, Patrick. *Glocalization: The Human Side of Globalization as If the Washington Consensus Mattered.* Lulu Press, 2007.

Mumford, Lewis. *Technics and Civilization.* Harcourt, Inc., 1934.

Murphy, James T., and Padraig Carmody. *Africa's Information Revolution: Technical Regimes and Production Networks in South Africa and Tanzania.* John Wiley & Sons, 2015.

Nkwi, Walter Gam. 'Cell Phone Repairers in Cameroon, 2000-2013.' *Journal for the Advancement of Developing Economies,* vol. 4, no. 1 (2015).

Nkwi, Walter Gam. 'From the elitist to the commonality of voice communication: The history of the telephone in Buea, Cameroon.' In *Mobile Phones: The New Talking Drums of Everyday Africa,* edited by Mirjam de Bruijn et al., Langaa Rpcig, 2009.

Nkwi, Walter Gam. 'Gender, and Mobile Phone Economy for Sustainable Development in Cameroon,' Journal of Sustainable Development in Africa, Volume 16, No.8, (2014).

Nyamnjoh, Francis B., and Ingrid Brudvig, editors. *Mobilities, ICTs and Marginality in Africa: Comparative Perspectives.* HSRC Press, 2016.

Nyamnjoh, Francis B. 'Married but available' in De Bruijn et al. *Mobile Phones: The New Talking Drums of Everyday Africa,* edited by Mirjam de Bruijn and Francis Nyamnjoh, Langaa Rpcig, 2009.

Oduor, Jacob, Kethi Ngoka, and Maureen Odongo. 'Capital Requirement, Bank Competition and Stability in Africa.' *Review of Development Finance*, vol. 7, no. 1, (June 2017), pp. 45–51.

Piot, Charles. *Nostalgia for the Future: West Africa after the Cold War.* University of Chicago Press, 2010.

Piot, Charles. *Remotely Global: Village Modernity in West Africa.* The University of Chicago Press, 1999.

Plato. *The Republic.* Translated by Richard Sterling and William Scott, Norton & Company, Incorporated, W. W., 1996.

Postman, Neil. *Technopoly: The Surrender of Culture to Technology.* Vintage Books, 1993.

Redfield, Robert, Ralph Linton, and Melville J. Herskovits. 'Memorandum for the Study of Acculturation.' *American Anthropologist*, vol. 38, no. 1, 1936, pp. 149–152. *JSTOR.*

Roberts, Sam. 'Influx of African Immigrants Shifting National and New York Demographics.' *The New York Times*, The New York Times, 1 Sept. 2014.

Robertson, Roland. *Globalization: Social Theory and Global Culture.* SAGE Publications, 1992.

Robertson, Roland, Mike Featherstone, and Scott Lash. *Global Modernities.* SAGE Publications, 1995.

Rostow, Walt Whitman. *The Process of Economic Growth.* W.W. Norton & Company, Inc., 1962.

Rostow, Walt Whitman. 'The Stages of Economic Growth.' *The Economic History Review*, vol. 12, no. 1, (1959), pp. 1–16. *JSTOR.*

Roudometof, Victor. *Glocalization: A Critical Introduction.* Routledge, 2016.

Sachs, Jeffrey. *The End of Poverty.* Penguin Press, 2005.

Sam, L. David. 'Acculturation: Conceptual background and core components,' in *The Cambridge Handbook of Acculturation Psychology,* eds. David L. Sam and John W. Berry (Cambridge University Press, 2006).

Samuel, Huntington P. *The Clash of Civilizations? The Debate.* Simon & Schuster, 1997.

Severino, Jean-Michel and Jérémy Hadjenberg, *Entrepreunante Afrique,* Odile Jacob, 2016.

Slater, Don, and Janet Kwami. *Embeddedness and escape: Internet and mobile use as poverty reduction strategies in Ghana.* London: University College, 2005.

Smith, Gerry. "Left to Die ... All for The Sake of a Mobile Phone'.' *The Huffington Post,* TheHuffingtonPost.com, 25 Jan. 2014.

Smith, Max. 'Mobile Telephony and Local Agency: Cameroonians Ways of Appropriation,' ISP Cameroon, 2016.

Smith, Stephen. *La ruée vers l'Europe: la jeune Afrique en route vers le vieux continent.* Bernard Grasset, 2018.

Stanton, Andrea L., Patit Mishra, Edward Ramsamy, Peter J. Seybolt, and Carolyn M. Elliott, editors. *Cultural Sociology of the Middle East, Asia, and Africa: an Encyclopedia.* SAGE Publications, 2012.

Steinmueller, W. Edward. 'ICTs and the Possibilities for Leapfrogging by Developing Countries.' *International Labour Review,* vol. 140, no. 2, 2001, pp. 193–210, 194.

Taussig, Michael T. *Mimesis and Alterity: A Particular History of the Senses.* Routledge, 1993.

Tchakounté, Franklin, Jean M. Nlong, Paul Dayang, and Njei Check. 'Understanding of the Behavior of Android Smartphone Users in Cameroon: Application of the Security.' *ResearchGate,* Sept. 2014.

Teske, Raymond H. C., and Bardin H. Nelson. *Acculturation and Assimilation: a Clarification*. American Anthropological Association, 1974

Tran, Khanh A. 'The Role of Information and Communication Technology in the Acculturation of Vietnamese Refugees.' Masters Thesis, University of San Francisco, 2013.

Van Beek, Wouter. 'The healer and his phone: medicinal dynamics among the Kapsiki/ Higi of Northern Cameroon,' in *Mobile Phones: The New Talking Drums of Everyday Africa*, edited by Mirjam de Bruijn et al., (Langaa Rpcig, 2009), 129.

Wadhwa, Vivek, and Salkever, Alex. *Your Happiness Was Hacked Why Tech Is Winning the Battle to Control Your Brain--And How to Fight Back*. Berrett-Koehler Publishers, Incorporated, 2018.

Wallerstein, Immanuel Maurice. *The Modern World System*. Academic Press, 1976.

Ziff, Bruce H., and Pratima V. Rao. *Borrowed Power: Essays on Cultural Appropriation*. Rutgers University Press, 1997.

Zweig, Stefan. *The World of Yesterday: Memoirs of a European* (Viking Press, 1942).